Older Women, Younger Men

Older Women, Younger Men

New Options for Love and Romance

Felicia Brings
and
Susan Winter

New Horizon Press
Far Hills, NJ

Brings, Felicia and Winter, Susan
        Older Women, Younger Men: New Options for Love and Romance

Cover Design: Norma Erler Rahn
Interior Design: Susan M. Sanderson

Library of Congress Control Number: 00-132571

ISBN: 0-88282-200-4
New Horizon Press

Manufactured in the U.S.A.

2004   2003   2002   2001   2000   /   5   4   3   2   1

Authors' Note

This book is based on extensive interviews of older women, younger men, their families and friends and experts in the fields of psychology, psychotherapy, social work and relationship counseling. Fictitious identities and names have been given to all characters in this book—except contributing experts—in order to protect individual privacy.

Table of Contents

Acknowledgements

We would like to express our thanks and appreciation to Marianne Strong, Mai Ding Wong, Linda Miele, Dr. Kathleen Calabrese and C. David Heymann for their wonderful support and without whom this book would not have materialized.

Our heartfelt gratitude goes out to all of the individuals who participated in our research and so graciously agreed to share their lives and stories.

Introduction

What's Your Fantasy?

"Share the fantasy," the old Chanel television commercial used to say. We reveal our fantasies in those endless checklists we keep making to describe the men we're looking for. You know the list we mean—the one that specifies that they must be attractive, kind, loyal, have a sense of humor, be faithful, professional, successful, affluent, intelligent, etc. Sounds familiar, doesn't it? But is it realistic? Is this why we're thirty-plus, forty-plus or fifty-plus and still looking? Hunting? Sometimes desperately? It's time for a reality check. Such men probably don't exist—and even if they did, they may not be looking for us!

To begin with, there are considerably fewer single, middle-aged men than women. Men who are widowed or divorced tend to re-couple quickly. Furthermore, the men who are single and available are often looking for women who are ten to fifteen years younger than they are (the trophy wife).

Certainly nobody should end up with a man who isn't loving, kind, faithful, honest and sexy. But some of our other demands and expectations need to be re-examined—not with a cynical eye, but with an open one (or two if we want to see clearly).

Born Again (This Time Without the Old Expectations)

As was the case with our beliefs in Santa Claus and the Easter Bunny, letting go of our old ideologies about how things should be is a necessary part of growing up. We should, in fact, be used to relinquishing the past by now, considering how much has already changed in our lives since those expectations were originally formed. Some of us watched television shows with role models that shaped our thinking: *The Donna Reed Show*, *Ozzie and Harriet* and *Father Knows Best*, while others saw *The Brady Bunch*, *Family Ties* and *Happy Days*. Despite those falling for *Who Wants to Marry a Multi-Millionaire*, women were changed by the feminist movement and contemporary life. This isn't a complaint, mind you. It's a good thing, but in the new millennium some other old patterns of belief and expectation must be exorcised before we can really come into our own. Powerful, independent AND a goddess is a brand new archetype that's emerged fairly late in most of our lives, so we have no solid role models (except maybe Xena the Warrior Princess, but because of television mores she is portrayed by a very young woman).

Most of us don't really expect a man to support us anymore. Still, we cling to the belief that he has to be a traditional peer in other ways. We want him to be intelligent and have a good (read "well-paying") job. We want him to be an "equal." But why? You might be amazed at the number of female lawyers, doctors and advertising executives whose construction worker, firefighter and cable repairman companions are making them happy and serene. Did we say *companions* instead of *husbands*? The need to be married is another belief that might, under scrutiny, be worthy of challenging. Don't panic! We are not saying don't get married. If you want to be married, you certainly have our blessings. It's just that if you're in your forties, fifties or beyond and you don't want more children, you might want to consider creating a committed, monogamous relationship with a man which doesn't necessarily involve the sharing of all your hard-won assets. Why create baggage? Haven't yours weighted you down in the past? Once again, let us remind you that we're not against marriage or even joint checking accounts. We are simply reminding you that other options exist and that modern women don't have to be locked into old patterns.

New family blueprints are entering the social consciousness at an amazing rate: single parent families, step-families, gay and lesbian couples-with-children families, interracial families and others. Remember, too, that each of these increasingly viable and acceptable families was initially met with scorn, social ostracism, criticism and family disapproval. *That's how it is and that's just tough if you disagree*, these new groups seem to be saying to the world. *We're here and you'd just better accept us.* Slowly but surely, most of us are accepting them. We are evolving, and that is why we need to examine the relationships of committed older women and younger men who are opting for ongoing romance. This type of relationship is simply another option for your consideration. It is, however, a different ballgame and does, very definitely, require an entirely new set of rules.

I'm Not Cher or Raquel. It's Not for Me!

What we want is often shaped by what we believe we can get. Men, no matter how out of shape, bald, impotent or poorly dressed, always seem to think of themselves as God's gifts to women. But even the most beautiful woman will question and doubt her desirability because she's not a size six or because she's no longer twenty-six. No wonder we accept and easily take for granted the older man/younger woman combination. Older men have no problem believing that they can attract much younger women and so they often do. Older women question their ability to attract younger men ("What would he want with me?") and so they habitually overlook or ignore a fertile land of relationship opportunity.

When we examine our fears in the light, we might just see that they are merely thought forms and not necessarily based in reality. For example: "I'm afraid a younger man will leave me" or "When I'm sixty and he's forty-five, he'll want a younger woman" or "Won't he be turned off by the changes in my body?"

Yes. No. Maybe. There are no guarantees, after all. Look at the marriages between men and women close in age that end in divorce because the man left the woman for these or other reasons. It does happen. Maybe you will want to leave him. That happens, too. There are no guarantees—not for you and not for your twenty-five-year-old daughter who's probably marrying (or living with) a guy close to her age. Keep in mind that women today are not the way women used to be. We are more independent. We work out, eat healthfully and take care of our inner and outer selves. We are a new breed. The women's movement has forced us to evolve, more so and at a much faster pace than men. Older women today are younger in heart, mind and spirit than our male counterparts. In fact, we have few male counterparts except perhaps among younger men.

What more and more older women are now discovering is that younger men often are as attracted to us as we are to them. It is a different game, however, and new rules apply, as do new expectations. There are things we need to let go of and things we need to open up to. Don't worry, we'll guide you. We have learned them through our own experiences as well as those of our friends and acquaintances. One more thing. We don't consider fewer than ten years a significant age difference. If you're fifty and he's forty-two, you're actually pretty evenly matched and we don't think that counts. Ten years or more is when it gets interesting, challenging and, most of all, very rewarding.

The Perks of Empowerment

There is nothing like watching a friend come to life and sparkle when she's in love. However, that sparkle transforms into a neon light when the object of her affection is a younger man. Men have always been allowed to experience this feeling as they've pranced around with beautiful, young things on their arms. "She makes me feel young again," he says, gazing at her lovingly.

We have seen women appear to reverse in age by ten, fifteen and even twenty years and radiate the most exciting, youthful, joyous outlook on life simply because their mate was ten, fifteen or twenty years younger. It's as though they are reliving a part of their lives that they didn't do justice to at the time. Perhaps they were involved with raising their children, helping support a man's career or working on their own career and simply experienced those hectic years on automatic pilot. The women we've met who have retrieved the joys of those years through their relationships with younger men are stable, rational, well adjusted, financially secure, intelligent and successful. They have their own status, their own money and their own identity.

Having always made choices for a particular set of reasons, we are free now to see if those reasons are still appropriate for future choices. We no longer have to choose a man because he's a good provider. We have learned to provide for our children and ourselves. We need not choose a man because of his status—we have our own. We have carved out our own social position and can create our own opportunities. We have often, in the past, relied on men for these things. A lot of the second marriages we've seen were also determined by the man's ability to adequately provide for the woman's children. Once again, the woman may have chosen not for herself, but for the security of her children. She has, once again, sacrificed herself. When the children are grown and the woman finds herself single again, she can now, perhaps for the first time in her life, make a choice that suits her, a choice based on what she wants rather than what she needs.

The good news is that cooking dinner is no longer a prerequisite task for wives. We no longer even have to raise children if this is not our path. Many of the things that seemed mandatory in the past have now become options. When we release our embarrassment and discomfort about admitting to the world that we are attracted to and/or have serious feelings about much younger men, we begin to see that the pool of available partners widens considerably. The parameters of choice expand when vistas open and when our needs are no longer financial, social or childbearing.

Older women/younger men relationships are a lot more prevalent than many people think. Because society still views them as inappropriate, unacceptable, tawdry or otherwise taboo, they tend to be hidden, not talked about much and often sneered at. They are not considered to be "A-list" relationships.

Too often these relationships are met with extreme criticism, censure and scorn, and are rejected by the couple's friends and family members. Too often these couples have been made to suffer for making non-traditional choices. If our purpose in life is—as we believe it to be—to give and receive love, that hostility needs to be released. None of us should have to suffer simply because we have chosen to love someone. This book is our contribution in support of our belief that this world needs more love in it, not less. For those who must project anger, censure, disapproval and rejection, let them aim it at the murderers, rapists and drunk drivers of the world rather than at people who simply choose to love one another.

Our own experiences, as well as those of many of our friends and acquaintances who are of mixed ages, tell us that these are very viable relationships and stand as good a chance as any to succeed over time. In conducting our research for this book, we have spoken to over two hundred individuals, including committed couples in which the woman was ten or more years older than the man. Both of us wished that we'd had the benefit of knowing these couples and learning from their experiences years ago so that we might have had more guidance for ourselves. These types of relationships are a newly emerging archetype in our society and we believe they need to be addressed and explored.

While we are not advocating romantic relationships between older women and younger men as a lifestyle for everyone, we are acknowledging the need for a manual—a guide to what to expect and how to handle some predictable situations. We would like to see more women expand their relationship options and we want to share what we've learned, sometimes pleasantly and sometimes painfully. We want to shed light on the pitfalls as well as the perks of these relationships. We want to walk women through the existing minefields, empowering them to release their fears and false beliefs in order to consciously make choices that suit them. If we advocate anything, it is opening yourself to more love, greater happiness and inner peace.

So hang in there as we take you through this brave new world of relationship potential. It's a ride you may well be sorry to have missed...so far. However, now that you're reading this book, we hope getting older becomes about increasing—not diminishing—the joys life holds in store for you.

Chapter 1

New Archetypes

Women should always marry younger men because men age faster.
Ruth (age 84)

Old barriers are being broken down all around us. Interracial marriages, single parenthood by choice, childless (by choice) marriages and openly committed gay/lesbian relationships represent examples of alternative life options that, unthinkable only a few years ago, are today becoming part of the mainstream. Nevertheless, all of them were—and some still are—met with resistance, derision and non-acceptance. However, the resistance is far less today than it was yesterday, as increasing numbers of people feel empowered to live their lives in accordance with their own needs, beliefs and values. The people who are entering these new territories and creating these new archetypes are, for the most part, sane, intelligent, responsible and productive members of society. Many of them happen to be older women.

According to Dr. Kathleen Calabrese, a Manhattan-based psychotherapist:

> *As a woman comes into her power, the greatest creative force on earth is unleashed. It is a woman's nature to create, to stimulate growth, to challenge status quo, but a young woman often does not understand this to any depth. She does not take this in as true about herself. It takes time and living life for a woman to be in touch with her power and to become willing to exercise it. This feminine power is born of wisdom, which develops well after work has begun, degrees have been earned, marriages have been launched and children have been born.*

1

The creators of these new archetypes are courageous enough to with-stand the often overwhelming pressure to conform to the old social norms and traditions, norms and traditions that just don't happen to work for everyone.

One of the most obviously manifest signs of an evolutionary change in the zeitgeist is in the new choices being made today by women. As women of the baby boomer generation mature, come into their own and exercise greater economic and political power, they are upsetting old traditions and creating new ones. Dr. Calabrese reminds us that today far greater num-bers of women than men are choosing to dissolve their long-term marriages to face the hazards of the unknown. She goes on:

> *Increasing numbers of women are choosing to live their lives as sin-gle women. One of the ways we know that women are beginning to see themselves as multifaceted individuals rather than simply as caregivers and nurturers of others is because more and more older women are leaving the security and comfort of their long-term marriages to live life in a more hon-est, autonomous way. This is an indication that the stranglehold of the patriarchy is loosening, albeit slowly and painfully, and a more inclusive, expansive, feminine energy is coming in to offer balance and wholeness to a fractured world. It will probably be another millennium before this evo-lutionary process reaches and impacts all levels of culture, but women are the pioneers of this great revolution.*

Older women/younger men relationships are far more prevalent and far more successful than society at large would have us believe. The theme that the social order reinforces often is the message that these relationships are a *bad* thing—and even under the very best of circumstances—are only a *tem-porary* thing. Popular movies, after all, suggest that it's perfectly okay for a man in his fifties and sixties (and if the man looks like Paul Newman, in his seventies) to court, woo and end up with a woman twenty or even thirty years younger. However, in those rare cases in which the woman is older than the man, such coupling ends badly, sadly or tragically. The truth is, we've been sold a bill of goods, one we're just beginning to realize is bogus. Our research for this book confirms that older women/younger men rela-tionships are an increasingly viable (dare we say common?) phenomenon. But many of them are "hidden" because of widely accepted perceptions that they are somehow less than high quality relationships. *Psychology Today* magazine recently featured an analysis of this situation:

> *Today, more and more women find the men of their generation stuck in an outdated patriarchal mode and the men of the next generation more eager for gender equality.*

Out here in the three-dimensional world, September-May relationships stand a good chance of working, if the aging woman can stop taking seriously the messages from the movies that tell her that men naturally want younger women. Real men want women of any age who like them, who want to make them feel good and who raise their testosterone level.

There is an enormous population of older single, divorced and widowed women (think baby boomers) who are repeatedly frustrated in their efforts to find appropriate mates. "There aren't any men out there," many complain. The "age appropriate" men they meet are too often far less evolved than these women or are threatened by the women's success or are in depressing physical shape or are themselves seeking women who are fifteen to twenty years younger (trophy wives). As if this weren't bad enough, there is also the fact that there are far fewer forty-plus men who are single to begin with. Men tend to re-couple quickly after divorce or the death of a spouse. And how about the much lamented recognition by many, many single women that "the best looking and most sensitive ones are gay?" Because of all the existing stereotypes, most women have never been open to the possibility of finding serious mates from the pool of younger men. Those who are open to it, however, are finding a lot of satisfaction.

Older women who choose partnerships with significantly younger men are an example of one aspect of a new archetype that is emerging. We have no role models and no one to show us how to successfully navigate this road less traveled.

Traditional relationships are tough enough to manage, even though for these we do have plenty of guidance and support. Still, they run aground. Look at the divorce rate. In creating a new relationship archetype, we truly are pioneers, with our courage, intuition and innate wisdom being our only guides. The pioneers who settled the Old West had to fight a challenging environment. Today's relationship pioneers, the creators of all kinds of new family dynamics, have to fight, in many cases, hostile friends, neighbors and family members. We are birthing something new, and the process of giving birth is often a messy business, bloody and painful.

When the age difference is an obvious one and the woman looks decidedly older than her partner, some people will feel free to stare and make rude remarks. "Oh, are you his mother?" they might ask disingenuously, knowing full well that's not the case. Since they wouldn't dream of being so overtly rude and even cruel to a couple in which the man is clearly older, here they are engaging in age, as well as gender, discrimination. It's like being back in the fifties when, even in sophisticated metropolitan centers, an interracial couple would be openly gawked and sneered at. Can you even imagine that being the case today? Interracial couples are a fairly commonplace sight wherever you go these days, and while some individuals still may not like the idea, they certainly don't (most of them, anyway) express their prejudice in such a public way. They wouldn't dare. Society evolves slowly and some people evolve even more slowly than that, but even they learn what they can and cannot get away with.

Bias crimes, for instance, are illegal in the United States today. Yes, they still occur, but the fact that they are illegal illustrates that the society at large recognizes these crimes as being morally outrageous. This recognition alone creates an environment in which fewer and fewer bias crimes will occur, as more and more people learn that the objects of their bias also have rights. This includes the right to be treated with respect in public. So take heart and fear not. Change happens. Most of us do evolve, some faster than others. These are, after all, extremes used merely to illustrate a point. Fortunately, older women/younger men couples are not typically victims of bias crimes, but merely of occasional prejudices, fears and very bad behaviors. Our advice? Be cool. Don't respond. Don't act out. Remind yourself that you are living a different reality and it's one that suits you just fine no matter what other people think. Their attitudes are their problems, not yours. Hold your head high and remember that you are not the one exhibiting poor taste by having this relationship. Those who are making snide remarks, pointing and staring are the tacky ones! Realize that you are being acknowledged by your young man as the beautiful, exciting, sexy creature that you are. Focus on the positives, on the good news that there is love in your life and that he is appreciative and good to you, and that he has the sense to value you as the goddess you really are.

Chapter 2

Today and Yesterday

After being with Claudia for five years, I was ruined. I couldn't stand talking
to a young woman all night. They were all so empty compared to Claudia.
Tom (age 25, referring to Claudia, age 46)

Some empowered women have, throughout recorded history, chosen mates as well as lovers from the population of younger candidates. These women, who have practiced medicine, entered big business and the arts and sat upon the thrones of empires despite the predominating male-driven cultures of their eras, have oft times hidden such relationships.

These days, many women we think of as having money, power and the freedom to choose less than conventional paths are often in the press. Known for their success, their beauty and their talent, all aspects of their high profile lives are covered by the media and paparazzi so that their choices of younger men rather than their counterparts become public gossip fare. Some of them are very familiar—Carlos Leon, the father of Madonna's beloved daughter, Lourdes, is a man eight years her junior. The tabloid media grotesquely repudiated Cher's romance with the man she has publicly acknowledged to be the "love of her life," Rob Camiletti, (the so-called "bagel boy"), because he was eighteen years younger than she, despite the fact that many male stars take much younger lovers and brides without scrutiny. There is frequent comment upon the age difference between Susan Sarandon and twelve years younger Tim Robbins.

In Hollywood, the older woman/younger man phenomenon is prevalent. Some notable couples include Jacqueline Bissett and Vincent Perez (he is twenty years younger); Juliette Mills, married to actor Maxwell Caulfield (he is eighteen years younger); Kirstie Alley and her thirteen-years-younger partner, actor James Wilder; and television favorite, Mary Tyler Moore, married to sixteen-years-younger Dr. Robert Levine. Joan Lunden recently married ten-years-younger Jeff Konigsberg and Courtney Cox has married her seven-years-younger sweetheart, David Arquette, while Joan Collins has long been happily domiciled with Robin Hurlstone, who is twenty-five years her junior. Collins has written about Hurlstone, with whom she's been involved since 1988: "he was much younger than I, which rather bothered me, but didn't seem to bother him at all." Kim Novak's husband, Robert Malloy, is seven years younger, while Raquel Welch married her fifteen-years-younger partner, Richard Palmer. Handsome Ralph Fiennes proudly shows off his significant other, seventeen-years-older Francesca Annis. Even Sly's mother, Jackie Stallone, married her nineteen-years-younger doctor, Stephen Levine, and Olivia Newton-John had a long marriage (now ended) to the ten-years-younger Matt Latanzi. The fabulous James Bond girl, Ursula Andress, had a long-time love affair with the younger actor Harry Hamlin, which produced a son. Lucille Ball married six-years-younger Desi Arnaz in 1940, despite warnings that "He's too young for you."

Audrey Hepburn's final years were spent in the company of Robert Wolders, a man seven years her junior. Of Wolders's relationship to Hepburn, biographer Alexander Walker, author of *Audrey: Her Real Story*, writes, "His fidelity to her would be her greatest aid and comfort as she entered on the last and most moving stage of her life." Before settling down with Wolders, Audrey Hepburn had been married to Dr. Andrea Dotti, who was almost ten years younger than she. The marriage lasted ten years. Prior to meeting Hepburn, Robert Wolders had been married to Merle Oberon, a woman twenty-five years his senior. Alexander Walker describes Wolder's marriage to Oberon: "They had several years of happiness together before Oberon's death in 1979. Though married, they behaved like lovers. They strolled hand in hand along the beach in Malibu. They sailed their yacht together off Catalina Island. They checked into small hotels along the Pacific coast of California, using assumed names, like honeymooners rather than husband and wife. When Oberon had to undergo a triple bypass operation in 1977, Wolders kept a sleepless vigil at her bedside."

The attraction between older women and younger men leading to satisfying relationships may be found outside of Hollywood as well. The writer Anais Nin was involved with Henry Miller and was forty-one years old when she became lovers with Bill Pinckard, age seventeen. At the age of forty-four, she became involved with Rupert Pole, age twenty-eight. They were together until her death thirty years later. Jacqueline Mitchard, author of the bestseller, *The Deep End of the Ocean*, is twelve years older than her husband. Writer Terry McMillan's man is twenty-four years younger. The playwright Garson Kanin married the considerably older actress Ruth Gordon.

Dorothy Parker, famous wit of the Algonquin roundtable, married Alan Campbell, eleven years her junior. Comedic monologist and actress, Ruth Draper, met the love of her life, Lauro de Bosis, when he was twenty-six and she was forty-three. And then there is Colette, whose many younger lovers included her thirty-one-years-younger stepson, Bertrand de Jouvenal. Not that she was alone in favoring a family affair. Back in the sixteenth century, Queen Elizabeth I, at the age of fifty-three, took up with the twenty-year-old Earl of Essex who was the son of her former favorite, Robert Dudley.

Another historic figure, Catherine the Great, had frequent liaisons with younger men. When her son, Paul, was born, it was unknown whether he was the offspring of her husband, Peter of Holstein Gottorp or of her young lover, Sergey Saltykov. After Paul's birth, Saltykov went abroad, and Catherine took on a new young consort, Stanislas Poniaowski. Later, she embarked on a third relationship with a younger lover, Grigory Orlov, by whom she also bore a son. The relationship lasted twelve years. In 1773, Catherine began an affair with the great love of her life, Grigory Potemkin, a man ten years her junior. But he was far from the last. Biographer Isabel de Madariaga, author of *Catherine the Great, A Short History*, writes, "As the Empress grew older, her favorites became younger." Queen Eleanor of Aquitaine, the most powerful woman of the twelfth century, married the eleven years younger Henry Plantagenet. Lest we jump to the seemingly obvious conclusion that only powerful women can opt for such an unusual and socially unsanctioned union, keep in mind that in his youth French King Louis XIV kept the significantly older Madame de Beauvais as his mistress. We know, too, that Mrs. Christabella Wyndham, the mistress of King Charles II of England, had been his wet-nurse when he was an infant.

In more recent times, notable women from all walks of life are known to have engaged in relationships with significantly younger men. Helena Rubinstein married Prince Artchil Gourelli-Tchkonia, who was twenty years younger than she. Adelaide Johnson, a well-known and much-admired American sculptress, married Alexander Frederick Jenkins, thirteen years her junior. Tobacco heiress Doris Duke had a long-term affair with jazz musician Joey Castro, fifteen years her junior. Margaret Eaton, the wife of a member of President Andrew Jackson's cabinet, married at the age of fifty-nine a nineteen year-old Italian dance instructor.

Another woman who chose a younger lover, Aline Frankau Bernstein, was the first American woman to achieve professional renown in the field of theatrical design. Starting with the design and creation of the costumes for numerous productions at the Neighborhood Playhouse, she went on to make her mark at the Civic Repertory Theater, the Theater Guild and in several plays by Lillian Hellman. Though her successful career spanned almost three decades, she became better known for her lengthy affair with the writer Thomas Wolfe, twenty years her junior. She was his lover and she was also his muse. The character, Esther Jack, who appears in Wolfe's novels, *The Web and The Rock* and *You Can't Go Home Again*, was based on Aline Bernstein.

Still another to choose a younger man, Adelle Davis was a very popular writer and lecturer on issues concerning public health and nutrition. Her most popular books, *Let's Cook It Right* (1947), *Let's Have Healthy Children* (1951), *Let's Eat Right To Keep Fit* (1954) and *Let's Get Well* (1965), sold ten million copies during her lifetime. *Time Magazine*, in 1972, called her "the high priestess of a new nutrition religion." A major contributor to the popularity of the modern health food movement, Davis was an early public advocate of regular exercise and balanced nutrition. In 1946, Adelle Davis married her first husband, George Edward Leisey, ten years her junior.

Dorothy Katherine Wright Liebes, a textile designer and businesswoman, has been called "the mother of modern weaving." Director of the Decorative Arts Exhibition of the 1939 San Francisco World's Fair, Liebes was the winner of numerous design awards for her revolutionary approach to woven textile designs. Hugely successful, Liebes' designs were used for everything from industrial application to upholstery, clothing and furnishings for homes, hotels, ocean liners, airplanes and theaters. In 1948, Dorothy Liebes married Relman Morin, an author and two-time winner of the Pulitzer Prize for journalism. He was ten years her junior.

These past examples attest to the fact that older women and younger men have been pairing up for a very long time, well before such relationships came to be perceived as modern. The women we have told of in this chapter have in some large or small way made history or achieved a certain level of fame, whereas many of the women we have interviewed for this book have no particular claim to fame. Few are especially wealthy or powerful. Sometimes they are not even physically very attractive. The voices that speak in this book are those of homemakers, policewomen, secretaries, insurance saleswomen, therapists and others. They lead normal lives, surviving both happy and not-so-happy relationships with their mates as well as their families, neighbors and employers. They come from every socio-economic level and every part of the world.

What has changed, however, and in some quarters, radically, is the status of women overall in our society. Whereas prior to the modern women's movement, empowered women were the exceptions—the anomalies among the general population—today they are becoming the norm. No longer does a woman have to be a movie star, a high-powered artist or artisan or ruler of an empire to qualify as being empowered and independent. Today, it is the woman in Arizona who runs her ranch after her husband's death, and it is the woman in Pennsylvania who, having left a long-term dead marriage, has gone back to school, completed her education and is working for an accounting firm, supporting herself and helping to put her son through college, or it is the woman in rural Texas who owns her own beauty shop, or the woman in northern California who operates her own consulting business, or the woman in Michigan who teaches in her local school system—having already raised her children and paid off the mortgage on her house—who fits the description.

Nor are these women out looking for—or accepting—a man who is not capable of meeting anything other than their sexual needs. These are not women looking for boy-toys. They are not swingers and they are not seekers of cheap thrills. Today's mature, empowered woman has worked very hard to develop her professional skills so that she and her children—and often her parents as well—can enjoy the comfort and security that thirty years ago she looked to a husband to provide. These are women who have learned later in life about being self-sufficient and solely responsible for their own and their children's well-being. These are women who have had to work on themselves, develop themselves and work harder than they ever expected to, just to survive. Unlike most of the men of their generation, they have had to develop extra inner as well as outer resources in order to be competitive in today's marketplace. Their jobs are not just additional paychecks to help cover the costs of luxuries, but instead provide incomes that can house and feed their families.

Today's independent and empowered woman wants a substantive relationship with a man. She is frequently an active participant in her community and sensitive to the general standards of behavior within society. She may have very traditional values and is not out looking for an opportunity to rebel and flaunt her freedom in any way that might antagonize her community. She would, in most cases, have preferred to find a mate in later life from among the pool of so-called "age appropriate" men—men who share her cultural references, men she feels she can "relate to." But a societal shift has occurred which makes that option simply not available for many, many older women.

No longer the sole province of the rich and beautiful, the recognition that new and different choices can be made is moving into the minds of women in the modern mainstream of life. The history that is repeating itself is the fact that women—with the confidence, wisdom, insight and sensitivity that accrue with age—remain as attractive and desirable to younger men as they always have been.

Approximately 85 percent of the women we interviewed had been previously involved in marriages or relationships with men who were, to some degree, emotionally and/or physically abusive. Having experienced neglect and unloving behavior, these women had the insight to recognize and appreciate a good thing when they found it. Interestingly, however, virtually all of them stated that they had initially resisted the overtures of their younger mates in the belief that relationships with them could never last. Patriarchal society may be responsible for this perception, but women have certainly bought into it. Older women/younger men couplings are much mistrusted and misunderstood—many people believe these relationships cannot possibly be anything more than sexual flings, for why on earth would young men (who could attract more nubile young women) choose women who have lost their only valuable attributes, those of youth and beauty? It's a mystery, but only until one finds the key with which to unlock this puzzle. Could it be that perhaps mature women have something to offer that is even better than youth and beauty? It's a hard notion to swallow for those of us raised under Madison Avenue's value-shaping influence.

And we all have, to greater or lesser extents, bought into such myths. We, too, came to our subject in the belief that long-term, loving, successful marriages and relationships between older women and younger men probably existed because the women in these unions had worked to maintain well preserved outer appearances. Sure, a woman who dieted religiously, dyed her hair, worked out with a trainer, invested in a nip here and a tuck there and endured ongoing injections of everything from her own body fat to substances derived from food-poisoning botulism, cows and human remains, could perhaps attract and hold a younger man, one of the prerequisites being she looked really great for her age. So, we have to admit, it was startling to us when we came across older women who *looked* their age, did not possess the most toned and athletic bodies and often went no further than having occasional haircuts to alter their natural appearance...AND were happily married or in committed relationships with significantly younger (and often very cute) men. What does this mean, we wondered?

What we learned was that it was about love, respect, appreciation and devotion, which these women were fortunate enough to find in younger men who recognized their more enduring attributes. It was the men in these relationships who felt lucky to have found such special women and they were perfectly comfortable showing this in a multitude of ways. Lou Ellen, a hardworking, forty-two-year-old police detective, told us about her thirty-year-old husband, Jay:

> *There are days that I come home from work so tired I can hardly stand up, and my husband will just lift my legs up on his lap and sit there rubbing my feet until I feel like I'm back among the living. Then he'll go out and bring home Chinese food so I don't have to cook or do anything. In the six years that we've been married, he has never once not brought me flowers every week. He just treats me like a queen, something no one else has ever done for me before. How did I get so lucky? I don't know, but I say a prayer of thanks every day for us having found each other.*

What exactly is it that these older women embody which keeps their young men attracted, passionate and devoted? From celebrities and queens to computer programmers and sales representatives, the older women we've observed have one thing in common—they know who they are and are comfortable with themselves.

Knowing one's self, having inner confidence and being fully developed as a human being are very attractive and alluring qualities. Over and over again, the younger men in our research reiterated, as if it were a mantra, "They know who they are." We knew this was an important part of self-discovery and personal fulfillment, but didn't realize until we were fully into our research just what a powerful tool for attraction these women possess.

If knowing who you are is a dominant quality in these attractions, older women mated to younger, admiring men are in wonderful positions in life. While much of society asks us to focus, consciously or unconsciously, on what women lose (our youth and beauty), the active recognition on the part of younger men of the real qualities mature woman possess is refreshing. While a young woman may have diverse interests, hobbies and a bright inquisitive mind, she is still in the formation process and may or may not become interesting and complex as her life advances in years. She is an unknown—still in the process of becoming her complete self. With an older woman, you know what you are getting. She has had time to formulate her opinions, experience the buffet table of life and draw conclusions based on wisdom and insight.

One of the more interesting couples we met through our research was Claudia and Tom. They met when Tom was eighteen and Claudia was thirty-nine. Their relationship began as a friendship. Like most of the women in our study, Claudia had no idea that Tom was attracted to her at first. She saw him as a charming, sweet and engaging young man. But Tom saw much more. It didn't matter to him that Claudia was twenty-one years older. He saw the beauty of who she really was and found himself inventing excuses to see her, visit with her and spend time with her in whatever way he could.

At Tom's very young age, he had his share of emotional problems adjusting to what, a year later, became a romance. Although Tom clearly loved Claudia and wanted to be with her, he was in conflict regarding what he saw as the normal things young guys his age "should" be doing. There were fights, adjustments and many ups-and-downs. According to Tom:

> *I knew I wanted Claudia in my life and not just as a friend. But so much of what she wanted was beyond what I could give her. I tried to do it, but I couldn't. She tried to give me my freedom, but it was difficult for both of us. Still, our relationship was like a magnet. We would try to break up, and something would always happen to bring us back into each other's lives.*

Seven years later, they are still together. Both of them are obviously in love with each other and it was clear to us that no matter what problems they encountered they had a greater desire to be together than to be apart.

Claudia explained that early in the relationship she had tried to leave numerous times and had, by her own admission, over ninety dates with older, age appropriate men. In their times of separation, both Tom and Claudia had actively tried to find other mates from the pool of potential partners in their respective age groups. Both had repeatedly come to the same frustrating conclusion—they enjoyed each other's company more than anyone else they met. Claudia told how difficult this period was:

> I really tried to get over Tom. I knew it would be in my best interest to be with someone who could be where I was in life—more financially secure and established. I did look and even tried dating services and the personal ads. The men I met were, for the most part, great people, and they were definitely into having a committed relationship, but something always fell short. They would have only a portion of what I wanted and that was it.

Tom described virtually the same scenario in his attempts to date young women. He would find one aspect of the many qualities Claudia had—her physical attractiveness, her wit, her success, her warmth, her brilliance—but he was convinced, after much hunting, that none of the girls had the whole package. He explained how being with Claudia had "ruined him for other women":

> After being with Claudia for five years, I was ruined. I couldn't stand talking to a young woman all night no matter how cute she was. My head hurt. They were all so empty compared to Claudia. I knew I shouldn't compare them to her, but I couldn't help it. It was like having the whole pie and then only getting one little piece at a time.

We couldn't help but notice this couple that had fought being together was as close as any of our married couples and just as devoted to one another.

The depth of an older woman and the many qualities she has developed over her years are a powerful draw. While this very interesting example of a couple clearly in love yet fighting their relationship fascinated us, we saw with great clarity the intrigue and complexity Claudia had to offer Tom, how very proud he was of her and how proud he was to be with her. Tom truly "saw" Claudia in her totality and, in his eyes, no other woman could compare.

The mystery of romantic connection is one that defies all logic. We have seen couples that visibly appear unsuited for each other yet bask in the light of each other's reflection. We have seen examples of what most people would describe as a physically unattractive woman, whose younger husband is oblivious to everything external, even bragging to us about her beauty. We have witnessed couples so diverse that their age differences seem the least of their concerns. Somehow, for these couples, their relationships work.

Another story of enduring love was told to us by Bobbie. She recalled the experiences she had as a young girl growing up in Long Island, New York in a very conservative Jewish Orthodox home. The emotional impact of her Aunt Sylvia's marriage to a man twenty years her junior was felt by Bobbie and her whole family. Although she was only a child at the time, Bobbie saw and felt a strange type of reaction, a reaction that wasn't adequately identifiable until she became much older. Bobbie vividly recalled this time in her life:

I remember when Aunt Sylvia first brought Allen to Passover. I was very young...maybe four or five, something like that. Allen seemed very nice and I remember he took a lot of time to talk to me and my brother. But I also remember this strange atmosphere in the house. Mom and Dad didn't really speak to him. They were polite and all, but it was just a very odd feeling. I remembered thinking they must have been mad at Aunt Sylvia about something, but I just couldn't get it at the time. We had always loved Aunt Sylvia— she's my mom's older stepsister. But, from that day on, when Allen showed up, things were different.

Subsequent visits from Aunt Sylvia to Bobbie's family's home became fewer and further between. When her name was brought up in conversation, there was an odd silence, then a sudden change of topic. Sylvia and Allen married a couple of years after that first family presentation and slowly crept into a life of isolation. Too young to fully understand her family's feelings, Bobbie described her feelings of admiration for her Aunt Sylvia and Uncle Allen's relationship:

When I got into high school, I would go down to Florida to visit them. They moved there shortly after they got married. I loved staying with Allen and my aunt. I knew he was younger—it was pretty obvious just to look at them together—but to me, they were just my aunt and uncle. They took me all over—shopping, the beach. We always had a great time and even way back then, I remember thinking that I wanted to have that kind of relationship when I got married. It was so easy to see they were in love...and they always laughed a lot. They played like kids, then they would get more serious and you just knew they really liked each other and they were totally in love.

Bobbie finally learned the truth when she was having an argument with her mother during her high school years. She was experiencing the first flush of puppy love with a gentile boy named Eric. When Bobbie told her mother she could see them getting married and being just as happy as Aunt Sylvia and Uncle Allen, her mother unloaded with a litany of shame and accusations about Sylvia and Allen's "sick and disgusting relationship." Bobbie finally heard her family's true feelings loud and clear: Aunt

Sylvia was a horrible embarrassment; thank God she moved to Florida; she was obviously mentally deranged and not a good influence on the children. From that point on, the Florida vacations stopped, but Bobbie continued to write and call Sylvia and Allen throughout college and her early twenties.

When Bobbie married at the age of twenty-six a man her family approved and admired, she received a call from Uncle Allen wishing them well. Aunt Sylvia had been diagnosed with cancer some months earlier and Allen, as always, was by her side.

The touching part of this story was revealed when Bobbie and her "perfect" husband divorced three years later. Though contact with Allen and Sylvia had been less and less frequent, Bobbie told us how she received another letter with a photograph of the couple:

I remember looking at this photograph of Aunt Sylvia. She looked so old...so tired. And she had a scarf around her head from the hair loss in her treatments. And I saw how Allen was holding her hand, so proud, so in love with her, and I just started crying. All I could think was, why hadn't my own husband loved me that much? We never had to go through the problems they did and he left me anyway. I just looked at their picture and it made me feel so empty. Allen loved Sylvia through everything...and I knew if I ever found love again, I wanted it to be like what they had.

We very much wanted to include Sylvia and Allen in our interviews, but when Bobbie contacted them on our behalf, they declined. Allen was working out of his home on a more frequent basis in order to take care of his wife, as her health was rapidly deteriorating. In Allen's own words to Bobbie, "Living through this once is enough." It was obvious that the pain of their families' censure and disapproval was still so intense that to recount their story would only once again open the emotional wounds.

Allen and Sylvia's censure by their families is similar to other stories we have heard of long-term committed relationships by ordinary, not celebrity, figures beginning twenty-some years ago. Although the climate is much more tolerant now, for those early pioneers the price was very high. They did not have the advantage of being outside of society's rules thanks to celebrity status or royal birth. They were regular people who came from ordinary homes and backgrounds and were viewed as social lepers for the choices they made. Their lives together were hard and the repercussions of the paths they chose had quite a cost.

Allen and Sylvia's story of devotion reminded us of Merle Oberon and her adoring husband. Through sickness and health, he was always there for her. These couples disprove the theory, "He will leave you for a younger woman." When there is a deep connection between two individuals, we have seen their willingness to go to any lengths to be together. That true, deep connection allows people to overcome obstacles that partners of convenience or conformity would not be equipped to transcend.

The average length of long-term relationships in the couples we surveyed was sixteen years. While a small number of our respondents had been together five to ten years, there were also a number of couples who had been together more than twenty years. Given today's existing divorce rates, where seven years is considered a "long-term" relationship, we reflected on the possibility that external forces in opposition to these couples may have actually proved beneficial to their commitment to each other.

In fact, looking at the social and familial climates many of our couples had to endure made us wonder: Could it be possible that the hostility expressed by our survey-couples' communities and families actually worked in their favor? Perhaps the feeling, "it's us against them," creates a powerful bond, strengthening already existing love and devotion.

External factors alone cannot create a long and enduring romance. The couple must feel deeply bonded through their own loving sense of connection and that serves as the centerpiece of the commitment. While external factors can create a tribal mentality of cohesion, if the couple is not truly bonded through deep love and intimacy, eventually the outside influences only serve as one of many reasons to separate.

The couples in our research clearly love each other. They express joy and devotion to their mates. In our opinion, society's disapproval could have just as easily flushed out the faint of heart. These couples exemplify a level of intimacy that has not only stood the test of time, but deepened in spite of obstacles beyond their control. In Bobbie's own words, "At least now I know what real love looks like...and I won't settle for less."

Clearly, the older woman/younger man alliance is not just a passing phenomenon nor does a woman have to be the ruler of an empire to attract or be deserving of the love of a younger partner. It seems only to be the scorn, rebuke, derision and ridicule that is heaped on this type of coupling by a male dominant (older male dominant) society that makes such relationships appear to be so shameful and worthy of reproach, even in these modern times. Particularly today, more and more young and middle-aged women are embracing their power. Mature women, having earned their status and their financial freedom, now can choose and take advantage of more life options. The good news is that they actually are available, if only we're willing to see and be courageous enough to accept such options.

Chapter 3

Developmentally Speaking: Men in Their Twenties and Thirties

I'm into older men now. No more guys in their twenties, it's too much work.
I won't consider a man unless he's at least thirty!
Justine (age 50)

It is said that age matters less to a couple the older you both are. This is true. The age difference is not so significant when you are fifty-nine and he is forty-six, or if you are fifty and he is thirty-nine. It's quite another story, however, if you are thirty-seven and he is twenty-three. The maturation process for men from their twenties through their thirties is substantial. Personalities, values and codes of conduct are fairly well solidified by the late thirties to early forties. If your younger man is over thirty-five, you have a much better chance of knowing what you are getting in your partner.

The Early Twenties
A young man in his twenties is still largely in a developmental stage. He may adore you and want to be with you, but still need to go through the turbulent phase of checking out his new independence. If you have the fortitude to be patient and the desire to play this one out, it can be very rewarding. However, we only recommend it for the most emotionally secure woman. This is an experience best suited to a woman who is fully invested in her own life, separate and apart from her young man. It requires someone who has a strong identity, a firm sense of self and great flexibility. Control is not an option here. An open hand and an understanding heart are basic requirements for the woman who becomes involved with a very young man.

Young men in their twenties get confused. They want you—then they aren't sure. The roller coaster can be a nightmare if you are too sensitive and too emotionally involved and invested in a particular outcome. Love a very young man with a degree of detachment. Love him completely—just don't lose yourself in the process (good advice for anyone in a relationship, but particularly crucial in this situation).

- Don't listen so precisely to his words. Since young men aren't always sure of their feelings, you can be run ragged with their ups and downs if you take them literally all the time. Men in their twenties are still figuring the whole thing out—they are still integrating and learning how to connect the appropriate words with which to describe their feelings.

- You know in your heart if your young man loves you. If he is sincerely making an effort to learn about you—who you are inside and what you need from him—you may receive the great gift of being his first venture into true intimacy. You have an important role here. Your behavior acts as a mold for how he will see women and relationships in general for the rest of his life. You have the honor—as well as the responsibility—of being his first real love.

His early twenties are the most difficult years to be involved with a younger man. If you are in that position, you have our blessings as well as our sympathy. Expect a bumpy ride, but not because of you or your involvement in his life. In fact, you may be the only stability he has right now. The problem is him. Everything is new—perhaps school, perhaps his first serious (or full-time) job plus the demands of making important life decisions. It's all new input for which he has had no prior programming. He is just beginning to piece together this new puzzle called "Life."

Andy was twenty-two when we met. I was forty. He was at a time in his life when everything was in turmoil. He didn't have a great job, he was still in school part-time—he really didn't know what he wanted.

I have a couple that I'm close to (both the husband and wife). He is seventeen years older than she is. He kept telling me, "If you can make it through the first five years, you'll make it." He was so great to talk to...he'd been there. We'd compare notes. It was all the same stuff. The twenties are just really tough years for many people and it's rough if you're with them.
Deborah (age 42)

He was so young—twenty at the time. What a mess. I mean, he was a bit of a mess, you know. He was fun and open to lots of things, but it was really hard in the beginning. He didn't know what he wanted. He was up and down a lot. There were lots of problems because here he was trying to have a mature relationship with me and he was still just a kid inside.

Suzanne (age 35)

There is, however, a huge upside to this pendulum. The fun, adventure and playfulness can re-ignite a long extinguished element within an older woman. She has the opportunity to see, close up, the world through fresh eyes. She gets to experience wonder—to take pleasure in simple things that long ago may have been forfeited for the sake of duty and responsibility. There can be a sense of untamed joy. Her young man is devouring life whole—inhaling each new experience. This provides a high voltage charge that can jump-start a woman's otherwise very orderly, settled and structured life.

The Mid-Twenties

By the time a young man is well into his mid to late twenties, things begin to even out. He's had a taste of the adult world and gotten some much needed life experience under his belt. He may already have had a serious relationship or two, which makes your job a lot easier. You no longer have to explain the basic rules of grown-up behavior in a partnership. You are now free to expand your worlds together. He probably has a foothold in his career and is beginning to get on his feet financially. The constant inner angst of the early twenties is over and he has a clearer idea of who he is in the world and who he can be with you.

I met Darryl through mutual friends in the early 90s. He was bright, charming, talkative and looked like he was in his early thirties. When he told me he was at Rutgers College, I assumed he was a teacher. I nearly died when I found out he was a student. He was twenty. Our relationship only lasted six months. We loved each other, but it was just too weird hanging out with his college friends. He was too young and confused to maintain a solid relationship, so I broke it off. I ran into him seven years later, and he was an entirely different person. He was grounded, clear and had a great job. We saw each other on weekends and then decided we wanted it to be more serious. It's amazing to me to see who he is now—the seven years made all the difference in the world.

Claudia (age 42)

The Thirties

When a man has reached his thirties, he's probably well on his way to becoming the kind of person he wants to be. His goals are set and many may already have been reached. He is more structured, confident and secure. He has a stronger sense of identity and can view you as an equal, albeit his goddess.

Developmental Overview

If you find yourself involved with a man who is in the earlier developmental stages, you should be conscious of being the essence of "woman" in his life, not "mommy." You are not there to teach him life's lessons nor to shelter him from his own experiences. Allow him to make his own decisions and support his choices when you believe in them. Don't do his job for him. Let him grow on his own without your constant advice and guidance. He will love you even more for it. Provide him with a sense of safety and security through emotional support and love—not money or opportunities you provide for him. Men love to achieve their goals on their own. They need to know that they can do it themselves—rather than have you do it for them. Stand next to him; don't be the wind at his back. He will be able to see you as a true partner in this way and you will have all of your energy to continue to build your own life for yourself.

Two things you'll need in ample quantity when loving a very young man are patience and humor.

- Patience: What seems like a mountain to him is a molehill to you. While he is still at the point of gathering information with which to meet his day-to-day challenges, you have gained knowledge, which, through your additional years of life experience, has been transformed into wisdom. His battles may seem laughable to you—you've been there, done that and come through on the other side. It may require the patience of a saint to listen to him complain about these little obstacles—but remember, you are a goddess. This is a piece of cake for you.

- Humor: There may be times when you step back, look at the situation (you, involved with this really YOUNG man) and just laugh. Yes, that's you in the middle of all this. You may own fur coats, stiletto heels and designer jewelry, but here you are, in heat over a guy in sweatpants, sneakers and a baseball cap. Keep a light heart and refrain from self-scrutiny. There's nothing wrong with you—you've simply entered a time warp of sorts. As you view yourself from this angle, take a deep breath and relax. It's an adventure and you are one of the first courageous pioneers crossing this terrain. You may not do it perfectly and you'll have your moments of doubt and uncertainty. That's okay. At least you've reached out for a chance to grow, a chance to learn and a chance to love. You are in the midst of a quiet revolution—an internal awakening to something new and untried. You are doing what you haven't done before and reaping the benefits of a new life that is truly of your making and design and one that suits you at this point in your life. Bravo! You are your own woman.

Chapter 4

Mirror Images

*I don't want to have to jump out of bed every morning to
run into the bathroom and put my makeup on before he
wakes up and sees what I look like without it.*
Catherine (age 53)

When you are newly into a relationship with a considerably younger man, you may be self-conscious about the looks you get from others. You may be wondering what they are thinking about the two of you. *Oh my goodness, is that his mother? Couldn't be his girlfriend or wife...No, it must be his sister. No, it's his aunt. But why are they holding hands?* Especially if he is fifteen or twenty years younger or has a "baby face," you may hear the following horrific four words: "Are you his mother?" These words are deadly and you may feel as though you're going to die right at that moment. The psychological devastation that follows can be much worse, however, and can last much longer.

The only remedy to this problem is time. The longer the two of you are together, the more you will feel like a couple. Eventually, you will be so comfortable with him that you will cease to feel self-conscious. The kind of ease you have with each other will then become apparent to others.

In 100 percent of the cases we've researched where those four horrible words were spoken, they came from another woman. Adding to the mean-spirited nature of this question is that slight pause before the word "mother" is uttered. Men seem to know better than to ask this kind of question. They seem able to pick up the vibes between the couple immediately.

I was at an auction with my boyfriend, Tom (who is twenty years younger than myself). The couple sitting next to us had brought their son—who appeared close to Tom's age. As the day progressed, we spoke to this couple. The woman mentioned that it was a smart idea to bring our sons, so they could learn the value of antiques and artwork. I didn't say anything. Then the husband leaned over and quietly asked, "So, how are you...related to that young man?" I proudly said, "He's my boyfriend." No shock on his face, but she looked like she was going to have a stroke. Funny, they didn't speak to us after that.

Valerie (age 41)

We were in a grocery store holding hands when an older couple passed us. The woman leaned over and said, "What a sweet young man, holding his mother's hand." The husband turned and looked at her like she was an idiot and as she pushed her cart forward to continue her shopping, he walked back and apologized to us saying, "I am so sorry."

Leslie (age 56)

Perhaps because they have never experienced with their own mothers the kind of energy or vibes romantically involved couples emit, men can tell the difference right away. What's more, they don't particularly care. They just chalk up the relationship to great sex and leave it at that. Women, on the other hand, might be coming from a somewhat more malicious place or so it sometimes seems.

Frequently, this dreaded question will come from a woman his age or younger. Maybe she's not intentionally malicious, just confused. She really doesn't believe that you're his mother, however; that's why she'll hesitate for a moment before she says the word.

Whatever motivates it, being asked this question is an awful experience. As you pull your ego up off the floor and desperately try to remember the name of that great plastic surgeon your friend knows, you are also scrambling for a response. "No, I'm not his mother" just doesn't quite express what you're really feeling. Whatever you choose to say is up to you, but here are a few retorts we've heard and liked:

1. "Do I look like anyone's mother?"
   Kate (age 42) *Looks like a twenty-five-year-old Barbie doll incarnate!*

2. "No...he's my lover." (Said with a BIG smile)
   Angie (age 50) *A good grasp of reality can be an antidote.*

3. "Oh no, his mother's *much* younger. I'm his girlfriend."
   Suzanne, a lawyer (age 41) *Leave it to a lawyer to come up with a great line.*

Clara, forty-six, and Tony, twenty-eight, were comfortable being a couple. Clara told us about the day they were holding hands and window shopping early in their relationship, when she suddenly caught their reflection in a window. She had been so involved in looking at him and admiring his youthful face that she did a double take when she saw herself next to him. Clara explained her intense reaction to seeing that reflection:

> *My God, I saw this old woman holding his hand. All I could see were my wrinkles and the gray streaks in my hair. I never thought of myself like that until I actually saw us together that day. He looked so young and I was mortified. I looked like his mother.*

The image in the window had nothing to do with how Clara felt inside being with Tony. They were a couple, happy together and involved with each other. Suddenly seeing that reflection in the glass, she became painfully aware of the age difference. She had never dated a younger man before and Tony, who looked very young for his age, was obviously years younger.

Clara said she even thought of ending the relationship. Her internal judgment of how she looked next to Tony was an insight that older men with much younger women wouldn't process in the same way. Whereas an older man might look with adoration at his young wife or girlfriend and consider himself fortunate, a woman will typically experience a drop in self-esteem compounded by self-doubt and recrimination. It's quite a double standard—one that we frequently impose on ourselves!

Why does a woman process this picture so differently? Clearly we have absorbed the societal message that youth and beauty form the sum total of a woman's worth. The internalization of these values begins early, with our power accruing in accordance with our looks.

Sadly, the connection of youth and beauty to our perception of our worth comes up a lot in our discussions with other women. It's a psychological reality that even some of the most astonishingly beautiful women we've met must deal with. Some find the courage to walk through that fear. Others think, *He'll look at me in the sunlight one day and he'll run away.* To women everywhere who think that finding and keeping a "good catch" has anything at all to do with youth and beauty, we want to say three little words: Camilla Parker Bowles.

Admittedly, Prince Charles could not be considered a younger man, as he is only a year or two younger than his longtime love, Camilla. However, in the world of trophy men, we believe that the future king of England ranks high. The story of Charles and Camilla has certainly evoked wonder and criticism and has for twenty-seven years outlasted some of the mightiest threats and challenges that any relationship, anywhere, could possibly confront. Camilla, even when she was very young, was not a beautiful woman. She has been more maligned, and more publicly so, for her lack of physical beauty than has any woman in history. One British tabloid published a photograph of Camilla standing next to her horse and asked its male readers to vote on which one they'd rather go to bed with. Camilla has had to stand much social censure not only because of her ongoing romance with a man whose wife was quite young, beautiful and loved by the British public, but because Camilla is neither young nor pretty.

We want to make it very clear that we don't approve of or advocate adultery. We don't advocate adultery for the royal family or for anyone else. However, if we are to fairly judge or at least understand, we must acknowledge that Camilla Parker Bowles has captured and kept the love of the Prince of Wales. Despite the fact that she seems to have rejected makeup and plastic surgery (which she could well afford) and, as far as we know, has never developed a relationship with a treadmill, Charles discarded his very young and very beautiful wife because he couldn't stop loving Camilla. Could she have qualities that Princess Diana did not? Are those qualities more important, at least to Charles, who could have his pick of beautiful women, than surface looks or youth? For both Charles and Camilla, they must be. They are clearly committed to each other—no matter what other people think.

Fortunately, after a while most older women in solid relationships with younger men cease noticing the visible differences and focus instead on the similarities. We have observed that this sense of shock and revulsion described by Clara after she saw her reflection with her younger beau usually occurs when it's the woman's first experience with a much younger man and only in the very early stages of the relationship. Still, as Camilla must know, it can be extremely uncomfortable, if not cruel.

Build a Protective Bubble

If you are a first time player in the younger man/older woman game, you'll need to build a protective bubble around yourself. The insulation you need is your ability to focus on yourself as a part of a valued couple. You belong there. He picked you. He could have made any other choice, but he chose to be with you. He loves you and thinks you are beautiful, both inside and out. If it helps, think Camilla.

By focusing more on your similarities rather than your differences, you will begin to accept the outer image as simply an image—it doesn't define who you are nor does it limit you. If this is your first relationship with a younger man, you may experience heightened sensitivity to the glances or stares from others. How incredible that women—in this day and age—must endure such a double standard and judgmental society. Movies that portray a fifty or sixty-year-old man romancing a thirty-year-old woman appear to be perfectly acceptable. Does that man, in a real life scenario, doubt himself? Does he scrutinize his wrinkles? Does he feel shame, insecurity and societal judgment? Of course not—it's not even a consideration.

The protective bubble in which you must envelop yourself is also a state of mind. If you already have it and none of this bothers you, great. You are ahead of the game. However, if you are sensitive to the outside world, we suggest arming yourself with some rational thinking. You deserve to be happy. You deserve to design your life as you like and if others don't like it—well, it's not their life and therefore not their business. Remember that you are making a choice that men have easily made for centuries. If it's all right for them, then it's all right for you as well. Society and public opinion will eventually catch up with this trend. In the meantime, remind yourself that your partner wants to be with you—no one is forcing him. Out of all the women in the world, he has picked you because of *all* that you are, including your age. By all means, think Camilla.

As more time passes and you internalize the feeling of being a couple, the outside reactions will ease up. Your own energy of thought, of feeling blended and a part of the life of the man you've chosen and who has chosen you, will unconsciously radiate outward. People pick up much more than we imagine from our inner beliefs about ourselves. When you are at peace, your outer world will reflect the same.

There will be those occasions, however, when someone will openly judge this union. It will happen from time to time. It's their issue—you will eventually be able to see it for what it is—and their stuff. Metaphysically speaking, what we focus on becomes our reality to one degree or another. So we suggest focusing on mutual love and respect, on being deserving of a loving partnership. The critical judgments will either pass in time or be far less hurtful to you. We promise. Just continue to focus on your responsibility to yourself and things in your world will begin to shift into a healthy balance.

Chapter 5

You Will Be Judged!

*I felt like a leper. I couldn't believe the things that people thought
they had the right to say to (not to mention, about) me.*
Natalie (age 54)

From the macro to the micro, from the outer circle of the country club to the
inner circle of the workplace, even to the innermost core of who you are, you
will be judged. Some people will feel obliged to sit in judgment of an older
woman who chooses her mate from among the pool of younger men. If there
is any part of you that suffers from the need to people please or an excessive
desire to fit in, you will undoubtedly be rigorously tested in this arena. The
more conservative your environment, the more intense will be the judgment. The older, conservative woman who has always been something of a
status symbol, the widely sought after guest at any party or social function,
suddenly finds herself being judged and criticized and her reputation compromised. She is forced to pay a high price for walking her own walk.

Samantha was on everybody's invitation list. She was tall, elegant, beautiful, sophisticated, world traveled and knew how to spend her sizable
inheritance with style and dignity. Then she made the choice to live with
Mark, a much younger man, at which point hardly anyone in her community would speak to her, much less invite her anywhere. Her phone stopped
ringing and she found that she and her boyfriend were in a world of their
own. This propelled Samantha into an inward journey where she had to
reassess her values and standards regarding the meaning of friendship.
Eventually, she developed a new set of friends and opened herself up to
new options. She and her younger man are still together as a happy couple.

Although it may be difficult to endure, social censure will flush out not only your character weaknesses, but your false friends as well. Remember that by choosing to be in a serious relationship with a younger man you have made what is to some people a radical choice and this makes them very uncomfortable. Your choice forces them to consider or reconsider their own choices. You have deviated from the traditional path, which in some circles is akin to heresy.

They were probably jealous, but how hatefully they behaved. I knew that they envied me, but none of my female "peers" had the guts to actually do it. What hypocrisy! They would drool over the lifeguard at the pool and make sexual comments about attractive young men they saw, but when it came to living it out, they didn't have the backbone to take the heat.

Lori (age 48)

Unfortunately, *you* take the hit. Tribal mentality is strong and can be hostile in its reaction to you. In these relationships, it's your reputation at stake, not his.

I felt like a leper. I couldn't believe the things that people thought they had the right to say to (not to mention, about) me. How dare they analyze, comment on or criticize my choice of partner. If he were my age or older, they would automatically be tactful and diplomatic. They would at least be polite. But somehow his being younger gave them permission to evaluate us as a couple. This would never happen to a man who chooses a younger woman.

Natalie (age 54)

I'm so tired of being judged. It hurts so much. Society—okay, fine, I understand. But when it comes to the subtle or overt put-downs from friends—I just go ballistic inside. Why is my choice inferior? I don't need to sleep with some old guy on heart medication who can barely get it up because I need his money! I don't need to be shown off at the opera, the theater. I can buy my own dinners and go wherever I want. So why in the world would I be "normal" or "acceptable" if I chose someone who has nothing I need?

It irritates me that people think there is automatically something wrong with a woman who doesn't want to sleep with a man fifteen years her senior. And how do we treat a woman who behaves like men have for years? We tell her she's sick. She needs to grow up. Do the right thing. Become socially acceptable. It's an outrage.

Estelle (age 53)

Of course, when a man uses his abilities as a free thinker to make a radical choice, he is invariably called brilliant, dynamic, a lone wolf or a forceful decision-maker. As usual, however, when a woman makes a radical decision, she's called things considerably less flattering. "Who does she think she is?" people ask. Her choice has offered up the possibility of a new option and this creates an uncomfortable tension in the existing consciousness. This tension frequently causes a push to evolve and grow, and change is something that we all have a tendency to resist.

We view the women we've researched as pioneers of a new movement in personal freedom. Making such a choice, both in the past and at this moment in our culture, requires some form of payment or sacrifice. This choice, therefore, demands high self-esteem. If you are strong enough and have enough self-confidence to choose what makes you happy, please do so. It helps to set everyone else free.

One way to survive is to recognize that the process of choosing personal freedom liberates you. It enables you to connect with your inner core of strength and recognize that solid place within where you truly reside. You will grow up. You will not be killed by any of this and you will surely become stronger because of it.

I had to really take a look at myself—there was so much backlash around our relationship. There were days when I really wondered if maybe I was sick or perverted. But I was so happy with Paul. I had to really focus on what was good for me—and he was good for me. But I got through it. I did eventually find peace within myself.

Ellen (age 60)

There are many different ways in which we learn life's lessons. Sometimes we are confronted with situations through our work, our finances or through challenging health issues in which we are forced to stand up for ourselves and show who we really are. The more often we do this the more self-affirming we become.

When you choose to have a relationship with a much younger man, people will not only judge you, they will inevitably make some assumptions; the most common assumption is that you're buying him for sex and that he's using you for money. Sound familiar? Oddly enough, we have observed that the more serious the relationship, the more bizarre will be the assumptions.

This may well be the first younger man you've been with, but when described by others, it becomes a plural rather than a singular situation. "She sleeps with young men," they will say or "She's into young guys." Suddenly they've got you with multiple sexual partners, as if you've hunted the supermarkets for stockboys and dragged them into a back room. Society at large seems to accept the notion of an older woman having a brief fling with the cute tennis pro or personal trainer, but can't deal with them as an actual couple invested with love, respect, commitment, monogamy and devotion. That's society's problem and we don't think it needs to become yours. We bring up these commonly held assumptions because it is only by being aware of them that we can resist the temptation to believe them ourselves.

What other people think, especially if the other people are a sizable majority, affects us. We may not consciously agree with them, but if they state their cases loudly and frequently enough they can make us doubt our own beliefs. We must actively resist this. Friends, family, neighbors and well-meaning associates may tell you that this relationship can't work out; that he's just using you, that he'll dump you later for a younger woman or that you're insane to believe that this is anything more than just a fling. We are all very vulnerable to the collective consciousness, because it activates our own deepest fears. If we buy into these beliefs to any degree, we will mistrust and doubt and ultimately end up sabotaging our relationship. We will have created a self-fulfilling prophecy.

Does the older man who is involved with a younger woman have to put up with all these doomsayers? Hardly! "Good for you," the world says to him admiringly. Remember, by being involved in a relationship with a younger man we have made a life choice outside of the conventions of the tribe. Let's not fall victim then to the pressures of tribal thinking and judgmental attitudes.

Keep in mind the dynamic that allows a younger woman to be attracted to a much older man. He may not have Tom Cruise's looks, a tight, muscular body or a head full of thick, "I-want-to-run-my-fingers-through-it" hair. What he does have (at least in her eyes) is power, sophistication, knowledge, life experience and vision. These are profoundly sexy attributes and we can certainly relate to how a younger woman would fall for a guy who embodies them. Why not allow ourselves to see that the reverse is equally true. We possess some or all of these qualities and young men think we're exciting because of them. We just need to remember this a lot more often.

This was a strong, really powerful woman. She took no nonsense from anyone, she asked for what she wanted directly and she didn't play any kinds of games. It totally turned me on. This woman's power was so sexy to me. She had money, position, made choices that I could only describe as wise and she absolutely flaunted all of it. She was definitely the woman of my dreams.
Larry (age 27)

I was really taken with Liz. She was a complete woman—powerful, sexy and confident. I wanted everything to be perfect. This woman was so different from anyone else I was seeing—she had everything I was looking for and more.

Paul (age 40)

I'd been dating "throw-a-ways"—you know, the kind of girl you see a couple of times and that's it. Then I met Paula. She was smart, cool and interesting. I could talk to her about anything. I never thought she'd take me seriously—as more than a friend. She could have any guy she wanted—why me?

Louis (age 29)

What to Do If You Are Being Judged:

- **Reassess your values.**
  If you find yourself the object of judgment and censure by your friends, we suggest you reassess your values. Are these the types of people you really want in your life? How important are these friendships if they don't support you and your choices?

- **Do these friends really care about you?**
  Do these friends care about your happiness or do you make them uncomfortable because you no longer conform to their rules? Are they only "situational" friends—united by a common interest or activity? Determine if the benefits of such friendships are worth the time and effort to work things out.

- **If they are real friends, give them time.**
  There will certainly be those friends and family members who are concerned about this relationship of yours, but their intentions are to protect you from being hurt. If you feel that's the case, give them time. As they witness the solidity of your relationship, they will probably come around and be accepting. However, those people who are not concerned about your happiness and are simply threatened by your choice will also reveal their attitudes in time. Listen to your inner feelings and respond accordingly.

- **Hold your head high.**
  We can't emphasize strongly enough the importance of holding your head high in the face of social censure and criticism. You have done nothing wrong and nothing for which you should feel ashamed.
  The thoughts you harbor about yourself and your relationship affect the thoughts and judgments of those around you. If you value yourself in the relationship and radiate pride in your partner, others will respond in kind. We've all heard the expression "As within, so

without." The more you feel secure and confident about your relationship, the more others will as well.

- **Back off.**
  If you find yourself excluded from the social scene of which you were once an active member, then back off graciously. Don't try to push your way back in. Let them come to you, which they will very likely do in time. Their curiosity will see to that!

- **Don't talk about it in detail.**
  Don't talk excessively about your relationship. You think it's great and of course you want to discuss the details, at least with other women. Use caution and common sense. Bite your tongue when in a non-accepting crowd. Information can become ammunition. Even if you were up until two in the morning basking in candlelight and hot oils for a night that you could swear created a tremor on the Richter scale, zip your lip. Be discreet. Some people will get jealous and twist every detail. Remember that you're probably the only one in your group staying up all night romping around in bed. Don't give others more fuel for their jealousy.

- **Be discreet regarding his employment.**
  Be discreet about what he does for a living if his career is not on an equal footing with your peer group. It's more ammunition that could be used against you. "She's living with an auto mechanic," they might whisper among themselves (particularly if you are in a profession yourself). Even "He's only in entry level sales" can be turned into a malicious remark.

- **Switch topics when necessary.**
  If people ask you direct and overly personal questions about the relationship, switch topics. "So, how are you and Jack doing? Does he still have that mistress in New York?" or "How's the diet going—have you started it yet?" Such remarks will definitely turn the attention away from you—at least for a while.

Again, we want to remind you that real friends only care about your happiness. They may be initially cautious and hesitant about accepting your younger man. This is understandable. Give them the time and space to discover all the wonderful things that you love about him.

Chapter 6

Who Pays?

He actually appreciated me less, the more I gave to him.
Caroline (age 45)

Who pays? The answer is very simple: NOT YOU. That is, not unless all you want with him is a brief fling or you really need to reduce your assets for tax purposes.

We've seen it over and over again and it just never works. *I have more money, after all,* the older woman thinks; *what harm can there be in buying him that little trinket?* In some basic ways, as progressive as we've otherwise become in designing our lifestyles, some things never change. Despite the fact that there may well be a financial disparity between you and your younger man, we caution you to treat him like any other man who is interested in you. Would you split a check? Then do it, but if not, don't, and never make the finances your sole responsibility. Even if he can't come up to your level in terms of fine restaurants, clubs, drinks or pricey haunts, accept what he is able to provide with grace. Do not run out and buy him expensive gifts and jewelry. You will appear (even to him) to be buying him.

When your younger man buys you something, no matter how small, be sensitive, be gracious and accept his gift with appreciation.

I was dumbfounded. For weeks before my birthday, Joel was all excited about the present he'd gotten for me. He couldn't wait to give it to me, saying he knew how much I'd love it, how perfect it was for me, etc. At one point, he actually told me that it was something for which I'd remember him rest of my life. You can imagine my anticipation. I knew that he had very, very little money so I wasn't expecting a diamond tennis bracelet or anything like that, but God, what could it be (especially on his profoundly limited budget)? Finally, the day arrived and I got to open my present, the one for which I'd remember him the rest of my life. Are you ready? It was a box of low-fat protein bars! I didn't know whether to cry, laugh or punch him. At first, I thought it was one of those gag gifts and that my real present would appear next. Wrong. This was my birthday present. We had met at the gym and were both into weight lifting and often talked about the nutritional needs of body builders and things like that, but A BOX OF PROTEIN BARS!!! So I thanked him (what else was I going to do?) and realized that I was dealing with not only a limited budget, but a seriously limited imagination, too. He was a really sweet, caring guy, so I forgave him. I still get a kick out of telling this story.

Marla (age 55)

Maybe your ex-husband bought you a ten-carat diamond for your anniversary and maybe all this young man can afford is a semiprecious stone or a bouquet of flowers. If he spent time and energy to get them, remember that it is an act of love and respect what that means to him.

Allow him the dignity of being a man when he wants to pay—even if that means dinner in a diner and a movie afterward. He will appreciate you so much more if you let him have the honor of taking you out. He knows you can eat in the finest restaurants; that's where all those successful older men can take you. But with him, it's about just being together. It requires no fanfare. You like being with him, therefore location and atmosphere shouldn't be your priority. If your younger man does happen to have money, by all means let him spend it on you. Men often express their feelings in this way. Say thank you, mean it and enjoy.

Don't be a sugar mama, lest you lose self-respect and his respect. If this relationship started out as the real thing, it will be ruined by your playing that role. (You should be the recipient of gifts and presents—not him). Being a sugar mama removes you from the adored partner role and catapults you into a needy, desperate, ready-to-be-hurt caricature of an older woman.

Human nature is a strange thing. As much as we'd like to believe that we treasure and appreciate a giving heart, the fact is that, given the opportunity, most of us simply can't control the urge to abuse.

I got tired of hearing him complain about the fact that he needed certain things: a calculator, new tires, etc. I finally went out and got them for him. I thought it would help him and reduce the complaining. Once I started this, he was like a bottomless pit—asking for more and more things.

It got to be a routine—then I felt used and set up. The relationship deterio-rated from that point on. He actually appreciated me less, the more I gave to him.
Caroline (age 45)

Excessive giving on your part doesn't necessarily indicate that you have a giving heart. It may mean that you are consciously or unconsciously trying to manipulate him. When a woman gives excessively, it is usually because she is afraid that she's not good enough. She believes that if she can provide him with the objects or opportunities he so desperately wants or needs, he will stay.

Yes, he will stay for a while. He will probably also become moody, distant, petulant and demanding (like a child) and cajole her to continue giving him more to appease him and make him happy. An unhappy cycle of imbalance begins with the woman's excessive giving. The man's affections waver and she falls into a downward emotional spiral as she begins to doubt herself—and him.

We interviewed a wealthy woman from the West Coast who gave her very young boyfriend a Mercedes AND a gold Rolex watch. As a struggling actor, he couldn't afford to maintain—let alone garage—the car so he sold it. He kept the watch, though, and it looked pretty classy on his wrist when he went out with other women. When he tired of sugar mama (because she gave too much), he settled down to marriage with a manicurist. But there's good news here, too. His new wife was eighteen years older than he.

Tips for Gift Giving

- **Refrain From Giving Gifts of Any Kind During the Initial Courting Phase**

  This period is his opportunity to court you. Let him enjoy the experi-ence. Don't give him calendars, pens, magazines or CDs, even though you consider these to be mere trinkets. Do not set up the pattern that he is to be the recipient of gifts. If you do, you will pay for it repeat-edly throughout the rest of the relationship. Yes, he probably could use a computer, car, credit card, new sofa, television set, bed, etc. So what? It's not your job to provide them. Let him get them himself. Give him a chance to become the man you would like him to be.

- **Gift Giving Should be Reserved for Special Occasions Only (Birthdays, Christmas, etc.)**

  We do not recommend gift giving at all during the first three months of the relationship. If one of these occasions falls before the three-month period, send a card. This may sound extreme, but trust us. Wait, exercise self-restraint and look at the long-term goal. There is a delicate balance during the initial period of adjustment between you and your younger man. The behavior you establish today will directly affect your future happiness; it's much better to encourage the expectation that you are the recipient of gifts rather than the other way around.

■ **After the Initial Courting Phase (approximately the first three to six months) Gifts Are Fine**

Here, too, use common sense and don't go overboard. Use your knowledge of his needs and his interests in selecting creative (not expensive) gifts. It's better to spend time and thoughtfulness rather than money. Several smaller gifts geared toward his special interests show that you care enough to acknowledge his passions. Collecting these items may take more time and demand some creativity on your part, but it will be worth it in the end.

While he is courting you, pay attention to and be respectful of his financial status. Let him take you out and treat you like his date. Remember that he follows the same rules as any other man who takes you out. You may be surprised by how much fun you can have going to the zoo or roller skating. Being open and flexible will pay off in unexpected ways.

■ **What is Appropriate at Holiday Time and Special Occasions?**

When Christmas and birthdays do roll around, don't spend only in accordance with your income level, especially if it is higher than his. Spend approximately what he would on you. If you buy him lavish gifts priced well beyond what he can afford, it takes away the specialness of his gifts to you. Don't rob him of his masculine role and certainly don't rob him of his incentive. If the money is burning a hole in your wallet, take yourself to a day spa and spend it on pampering yourself. If you buy him expensive gifts, it burdens him with the pressure of having to buy you something extravagant just to keep up or save face. This will only build resentment.

When a man really loves you, he will save for months to get you something special. His biggest complaint will be that he didn't know what to get you, because, to him, you already have everything. Tom, age twenty-four, bought Rita, age forty, a beautiful bronze statuette of a woman with a leopard caressing her leg like an adoring kitten. He told her that was how she looked to him, beautiful, gracious and elegant. Perhaps he saw himself as the smitten cat. An auto mechanic, Tom spent four months salary on that gift. He had struck a deal with the gallery owner to begin paying for it well before Christmas so that it could be under the tree in time. Would you spend four months salary on anyone? Probably not. Enjoy being the recipient; it's a better position to be in.

■ **Creative Gifts**
Give him gifts that are either creative or experiential. Creative gifts (which take his interests and hobbies into account) might include a book on football, a video on bodybuilding, a subscription to a magazine he really likes or anything that shows that you've noticed what is important to him. After seven months of dating each other exclusively, Linda, forty-six, got Tony, twenty-nine, Christmas presents that reflected his many diverse interests: A CD for meditation, a book on the therapeutic use of herbs, an aromatherapy candle and a book on bodybuilding. It took her time to seek out each one of these items, but what it showed Tony was that she knew what was important to him and supported those things. He was very touched, as he was by the lovely card that she made for him.

■ **Experiential Gifts**
An experiential gift is simply an experience that you and your younger man can share. If you both enjoy hiking, how about spending a day in the country? Perhaps you could go on a picnic or spend an evening at the theater if there is a show you're both eager to see. Go away for a weekend to some place romantic that he could not afford to take you, but where you would both like to go.

The experiential gift is a chance for you to enjoy your time together and to share a treasured experience. As we look back on our lives, it's hard to remember every gift we've been given for holidays and special occasions. We do remember, however, our special experiences, like those great vacations or horseback riding trips on the beach or the way the sun set on that spectacular golf course by the ocean's edge. Experiential gifts are planned and tailored not only to his special interests, but just as importantly, to yours. Do something that's comfortable and fun for both of you. As far as embarking on a longer vacation together, we suggest that you consider it only after the relationship has been very well established and he is on an equal footing with you in terms of his commitment and contribution to the union.

The point is to minimize the discrepancy between your income and his. But if you are fortunate enough to have a younger man who is very successful, congratulations! You can still give him creative gifts that honor his uniqueness and areas of interest, as well as carefully thought out experiences. Remember, even if he is very substantial financially, that does not give you permission to shower him with gifts! Don't take the privilege of being a woman away from yourself. Instead, give him the opportunity to experience a woman's happy response to a generous man.

Chapter 7

Resist Becoming "The Source"

I learned my lesson with this one. I took care of him, gave him what he wanted and he ended up hating me for it. I'll never do that for a man again—of any age!
Sandy (age 56)

For many of us women, giving and taking care of others' needs has been a way of life. We have been nurturing, supportive and always there for someone else. It is part of our nature AND it is learned behavior, but at this point in our lives it becomes necessary for us to learn how to receive. Receiving is as important as giving. It is an intrinsic part of the same cycle. Unfortunately, our society has established an unspoken law that giving is good and receiving is bad.

Have you ever tried to give somebody something you really wanted them to have, only to have them turn it down? Do you remember how crushed you felt? You were denied the pleasure of giving because they were unable to receive. We believe in setting up a complete circle of energy with our mates. Chances are you've spent the last twenty or thirty years of your life giving of your time and energy to your children, husband, local charities, your community and the arts. Try something new: Learn to accept.

We understand that it is tempting to want to provide your young man with all the material things and opportunities he needs and wants. It's so easy for you to do, but, in the end, you'll resent feeling like his caretaker.

He made so little money it was ridiculous. After he paid rent, he literally didn't have enough left over to eat decently. What could I do—not feed him? I felt so badly for him. So after work he'd come over and I would make

36

dinner. At first it was only occasionally, but before I knew it I was feeding him every night. Now, mind you, I'm not a woman who cooks for herself, but here I am cooking—every night—for him. Something was definitely wrong with this picture. Even when he came over on weekends during the day, he'd ask for something to eat and I'd give it to him. I remind you—I DO NOT COOK!—but here I am, cooking, shopping for food, seeing to it that his needs are met. My resentment just grew and grew until one day I looked at him and realized that I couldn't stand being with him another minute. I hated him. I just couldn't stand him or the relationship another second. I had to get out.

Alicia (age 44)

It's not your job nor your responsibility to take care of your younger man. By caretaking him, you emasculate him and set yourself up to be "the source." When you set yourself up as "the source," you teach your young man to come to you out of need not desire and certainly not out of love. He learns that you are the one who fixes everything, takes care of all his problems, gets him out of jams, eases his life and supplies him with otherwise unobtainable opportunities and luxuries. This is not a great position for you to be in. It's bad enough if his mother finds herself in that role, but it's utterly disastrous for your romantic relationship if you do.

Setting yourself up as "the source" creates an energy drain on you from the very beginning. You are the giver—whether of knowledge, connections or money. You also set him up to be the perpetual taker. These roles become locked positions that remain fixed throughout the relationship. It will never result in partnership. Let somebody else fill those shoes. If you feel the necessity to "buy" him or in any way take care of him in order to keep him, you are in trouble.

The foundation of our relationship was built on a transfer of information—spiritual, psychological and business/life oriented. Jeff needed me to provide these things for him, to teach him about everything. I was so smitten with him that I took on the role of teacher, therapist and career counselor. I thought I was helping him and that it showed my love. It took me five years to realize I had created a Frankenstein. I was so eager to give him what he needed, because (as I realized later) it made me feel needed. The cost to me was tremendous. I sacrificed too much time and energy. I made Jeff and his development my project. That was the role he wanted me to play, but the price was my own emotional well-being.

The more I gave, the more Jeff took. When I tried to hold back a little, he became abusive, expecting me to be the endless provider. It leaked into every aspect of our relationship. I see now, in retrospect, that I was afraid if I stopped giving, he'd leave. Well, Jeff did leave, after he cleaned me out. What I learned was that my over-helping him made him resent me, made him

believe that he couldn't do it on his own. He ended up hating me. The pain
of this experience was incredible.

Pamela (age 42)

Being needed can be seductive, but it inevitably backfires. It is an unfortunate aspect of human nature: We tend to want what we can't have and to value what is hard to attain. This seems to be especially true for men. Perhaps it's even genetic. You are not endearing yourself to him by making yourself "the source." You are setting up a nightmarish scenario that will recur throughout the relationship, until you end up broken hearted and feeling empty.

He wanted to be an actor and I was very well connected with casting
people. I wanted to see him happy and successful (I would have loved for him
to make enough money to take me someplace nice).

I got him some "extra" work and that completely went to his head. He
became cocky and very condescending. He actually told me that he didn't
need me now that he was a "star." One night in bed, we had a bad fight. He
turned to me and said, "You're just jealous of my success—because you're old
and washed up!" I looked in his eyes and laughed to myself, knowing his
work as an extra would probably end up unseen on the cutting room floor. I
mentally reminded myself that I was leaving in two weeks for a role in a fea-
ture film.

Corrine (age 42)

I helped Tom with a major business deal. I knew the ropes; I've done
this work for years. He really wanted this client, so I walked him through
every step of the process. He listened, even though his ego was taking a beat-
ing. The client was definitely interested, but then there was some block to the
deal. I told Tom that we should all have dinner together.

Bottom line—I closed the deal. I knew I could do it. But that's exactly
when our relationship began to unravel. I got him what he wanted, but then
he turned on me. All of a sudden, he was mean and cold to me. It was very
confusing. I thought he'd be so happy. I learned my lesson with this one. I
took care of him, gave him what he wanted and he ended up hating me for it.
I'll never do that for a man again—of any age!

Sandy (age 56)

The one who always gives is rarely allowed to receive in this type of arrangement. If you are the safe supplier of energy, opportunity and gifts, what happens when you need a little support? You've given the appearance of invincibility so don't be surprised if support for you is lacking when you find you are in need.

Being "the source" is not kindness, it's control. The unconscious thought is that if you provide everything this young man needs, he will keep coming back. The motivation is fear and it reeks of low self-esteem.

It is very tempting to be the "big shot" with a younger guy. There's usually so much that they need—and so much more that we know. It is very seductive, but it is a trap. It feels good initially, because we're on a pedestal, but we also put ourselves in the position of being toppled over. At this point in our lives, we don't need to be anything other than ourselves. If men want to be with us, they want to be *with us*, because of who we are. We don't need and shouldn't want to take care of them. We may be getting older, but we are not getting desperate.

We must continue to be vigilant about guarding our often vulnerable self-esteem. We must also practice considerable self-restraint. While we recognize that the experience factor we have to offer is one of the qualities that make us so attractive to younger men, we must discipline ourselves to not give away or unduly exercise all of our power.

Chapter 8

Too Young or Just Too Wrong?

*Frankly, he was the best con man I'd ever met. Every
abuse was countered with "I'm learning" or "I didn't know."
I believed it! I thought he was too young to be so good
at manipulation. I totally underestimated him.*
Jessica (age 46)

When men behave badly, women often make excuses for them. We sometimes do this almost automatically, but especially so when the man is a lot
younger. "He's just scared of commitment," we tell ourselves or "That's normal for someone his age." "He just doesn't know any better, but I'll teach
him," we say or "That's how his generation does things." Wrong. Bad,
unloving or disrespectful behavior is not excusable, even for the youngest
of men. When a man cares for a woman, no matter what the age or age difference, he shows her that he loves her by being courteous and respectful.
A woman, whatever her age or circumstances, should expect and tolerate
no less.

Some men, no matter what their age, are simply *too* wrong. Signs that a
man is *too* wrong are things like his consistent trampling of your boundaries, lack of consideration for anything that has to do with you, narcissism
and involvement with his pleasures and needs only without regard for
yours. If these patterns exist in your relationship, we suggest you get out of
it quickly. Too often women attribute bad behavior to youth and thus
excuse it.

Some examples of bad behavior that women excuse because they think he's just too young to know better:

- After you've had sex with him for the first time, he doesn't call you the following day.

- He "disappears" for an entire weekend, doesn't call you, doesn't respond when you page him and tells you—days later—that he couldn't call you because he was busy.

- He uses derogatory language when talking about other women.

The problem may not be simply that he's young, it may just be that he's a certain type of man. Many highly informative books have been written about men who can't love, can't commit, can't be honest and can't be faithful. From these ideas and our research, we've come up with the following recommendations to help you recognize if you are in a relationship with this type of man:

1. State what you want and need from him.
2. Determine if he is willing and able to give it to you.
3. Observe his actions.

There are many books on this topic, but all of them, in one way or another, advocate the importance of these three crucial steps to help you assess whether or not this relationship can work out.

When a boundary has been trampled, an insensitive comment made or hurtful action taken, what should you do? First of all, we believe you should express your feelings honestly instead of secretly hanging on to anger and resentment. Honor your self-worth by stating clearly what you need and expect and the reasons why. People of all ages do better with explanations than with attacks. This approach works especially well with men. They don't like to be reprimanded, scolded or subjected to indirect or manipulative efforts to control their behavior.

First and foremost, you want to know who you're really dealing with here and, unfortunately, he's not telepathic. He can't read your mind. If you want to know how willing and able he is to meet your needs, you must express them to him openly. If he does something that makes you feel badly, let him know directly. A simple and direct formula we like to use reads as follows:

I feel _____ when you _____,
because _____. I need you to _____.

This is a widely accepted communication model that has been proven successful, primarily because the focus stays on your feelings and what you need. You make no personal attack on your partner. It is clear, to the point and instantly understandable to your listener.

Once you've stated what you feel and what you need—sit back and observe his reactions. Watch his behavior. It will tell you if he's willing and able to make the changes you require.

Willing and Able

Is the young man with whom you are involved willing to make changes in his behavior in order to improve the relationship? Is he willing to acknowledge your feelings? Willing to listen? Willing to include you in his life? Willing to be sensitive? Willingness means that he wants to do what is necessary for the partnership to work. The willingness to change, to make behavioral or attitudinal adjustments for the good of the relationship is the sign of a good man, whether young, middle-aged or older.

Able means he can take the information from the willing mode and consistently succeed in executing the changes needed. Not only does he understand what you have stated you want and need, but he is able to follow through most of the time (nobody's perfect, but you know when someone is making an honest effort.) Able means he has the knowledge and self-discipline to work toward achieving a relationship dynamic that will be successful for both of you.

Willing and able must go hand in hand. Sometimes a man is willing, but simply unable. This is unfortunate. He tries, but can't seem to succeed. He really wants to be with you, wants to please you and tries hard, but he always fails. Maybe the man is too young or maybe it's just his nature. If a man is very young, he is probably battling many other issues and the work required to achieve a healthy intimate relationship is simply beyond his present ability.

>   *He tried hard. I see it now that we're apart. He really wanted to be the perfect guy for me, but he was too young. He didn't know who he was, what he liked, what he wanted or what he believed. He just sort of picked up pieces of information from people—and from me—and then tried them on for a while, like clothing. It was never him. It wasn't real, because he wasn't real yet.*
>   **Christine (age 37) talking about Glenn (age 25)**

The worst scenario is a man who is able, but unwilling. This means that even if he is young, he is unwilling to be flexible. He is perfectly able to do what is needed in the relationship. He understands what you're saying and he understands what your needs are—he's just not willing to do anything differently.

Dealing with an unwilling man is a no-win situation. He is not a man who can work in partnership. He will not make you a priority in his life. There is no solid foundation for a relationship with this type of man. You will be chronically frustrated and dissatisfied. Age might be a factor, but it's not worth compromising your self-esteem waiting for him to mature.

We have seen women we know try to change the bad characteristics of men who are just *too* wrong. They work industriously trying to enlighten these men. We believe that people have a core and their interpersonal behaviors flow from this core. If you think about how difficult it has been to change something in your own core personality despite your fierce desire to do so, imagine the futility of trying to change a person who has little or no motivation beyond the pressure you exert. A man is either loving or he is not. He is either sensitive or he is not.

In our opinion, this has little to do with age; it is an inherent characteristic of the individual and there is nothing you can do to change it. Nor should you waste your precious time and energy trying to.

What we do find, however, is that younger men tend to be more open to subtle types of correction and are more flexible. A man at age fifty makes a conscious error when he stands you up, but when he's in his twenties he may really have forgotten, being overwhelmed with other things. We are not suggesting that you accept this behavior or make excuses for him, but at twenty-five he may not realize the importance of keeping his word. You will need to educate him about the responsibilities inherent in having an adult relationship.

Usually, young men will be accepting of this information. If they really did forget, they will make sure not to do it again. Watch for the consistency, or lack thereof, in their behavior. If you find yourself having the same arguments over and over again, then they probably are not going to change. In which case, even if they are young, they are still *too* wrong and they will be just as wrong when they are older.

We advise you not to get lulled into the "He'll change" trap. We have observed several of our friends and acquaintances go into heavy denial and suffer in obviously abusive relationships, while they cling to the wishful thought: *He's young, he'll change.* Being young is not an excuse for bad behavior. It does, however, allow for the ability to make mistakes from lack of experience. There's a big difference here. Observe how he treats his family and his friends. Think about how he treats you. You should be his priority. Your feelings should come first.

If you tolerate bad behavior in your relationship with a younger man, you are basically teaching him that it's all right to abuse you. We teach people how to treat us by how we treat ourselves. If you teach him by your acquiescence that it's all right to cancel your plans at the last minute to go off with his friends, for example, consider that you have confirmed a pattern that is actually unacceptable to you.

Rebecca told us about a litany of abuse in her four-year relationship with Hal. He was twenty years younger and the quintessential example of an abusive man.

It was the Fourth of July. I love fireworks and we had a date to go together and watch them being set off. The plans had been made weeks before. Suddenly, he calls, says he can't go, he's going to a party. He says he wants to be with people his own age, he's tired of feeling "married." I was left to watch the fireworks by myself. I cried all night. I couldn't even reach him to vent my anger, because he'd called from a pay phone. He didn't come home until four in the morning. I can't believe I lived with him another two years after that. I can tell you hundreds of incidents like that one. I would yell and scream, we'd fight and then make up. It would start all over again next time. He kept on and on with the "I'm young" thing. He needed to do these things, I was oppressing him and all the rest. It never got better, only worse. There would be good times for a while when he seemed to be getting it, then the whole thing would blow up in my face. I should have gotten out, but I didn't. It's taken a lot of time to get myself together. I couldn't see it for a long time, you know, and I didn't get out, I didn't stop it. I just yelled a lot, but nothing ever changed.

Rebecca (age 47)

It was a really big day for both of us or so I thought. After two years of living together, today he was buying me a ring. He had a brief family obligation, then he was coming back to pick me up at noon. Noon came and went. I paged him again and again—three o'clock, four o'clock. I was fuming by this time. Every possible thought went through my head. Finally, he shows up at half-past six in the evening when the stores were closed. I was in agony. His excuse? He was having fun playing volleyball with his cousins and forgot. He said I was neurotic. This kind of stuff happened over and over. I went up and down on a daily emotional roller coaster with him. I'd break it off and he'd plead with me to give him another chance—tears and all. What an actor. "This is my first relationship" and "I didn't know" and "I love you, I'll never do it again."

Broken dates, broken promises and now I had a broken heart. Eventually, he even needed to "experience someone new." He kept justifying everything because of his age, saying he "had to do it, you don't understand... you're the one with the problem."

I finally got out, but what a mess. I'm still distrustful of men because of this experience.

Dawn (age 38)

He played me beautifully. I was a savvy city woman experienced in the ways of the world and aware of human nature. He was a young, supposedly naïve country boy. Frankly, he was the best con man I'd ever met. The age thing really threw me for a loop. I totally underestimated him.

Every abuse was countered with "I'm learning" or "I didn't know." I believed it! I thought he was too young to be so good at manipulation, but I learned way too late he used his youth to rationalize living like a single guy with no responsibilities while in a relationship with me.

Jessica (age 46)

I'd never been involved with a much younger guy before—so it weakened my defense system. I believed his lies and trusted his word. How could he be so conniving as to do all these things purposely? He's so young, I thought. Maybe he's just confused or doesn't know better. Finally, after a year of turmoil, my friend set me straight. She said, "Rachel, he's lived it. He's lived with a family that lies and manipulates—he's a pro." She was right. Age was irrelevant.

Rachel (age 43)

I've learned from bitter experience that young doesn't mean innocent or unsophisticated or uncalculating.

Miranda (age 41)

If you find yourself constantly having to struggle and fight over situations like this, please realize that it won't get better. This is how this particular man is built; being selfish and abusive is not just a phase. Cut your losses, don't waste any more time, and then take a big time-out to re-evaluate your role in this unfortunate relationship.

How can you tell if a man is genuinely interested in learning better behavior and truly regrets his transgressions? When you present the information to him, observe his reaction. Is he extremely defensive? Or was he totally taken by surprise and had no idea that his actions hurt you? If the situation is explained to him clearly and very specifically, without anger or aggression, he will be better able to hear you. If he loves you and wants a meaningful relationship with you, he will respond sincerely and seek a meeting of the minds. He will want you to be happy. He will either show signs of interest in changing poor behaviors or express an offer of compromise so that his needs can be met as well as yours.

Bad behavior is intolerable whether it's in a man of twenty-one or a man of fifty-one. With a younger man, however, it's harder to tell if it's just inexperience and lack of awareness, as opposed to self-indulgence, resentment or simply unkindness. All the more reason to be able to state your needs directly and then observe his willingness and ability to meet them.

He kept saying that he didn't understand, he didn't know, he'd never been in a real relationship before. I mean these were pretty basic things, like we live together, you sleep with me, but you want to go out to clubs to meet other women? I couldn't believe I had to explain to him that this was not appropriate. He kept defending his behavior and doing the same types of things, but in different ways each time. He kept saying that he didn't know, he was just learning and I should give him a break. But everything he did (or wanted to do) was way out of my comfort level. It never got any better. I had to leave him.

Ann (age 38)

If your young man continues to excuse his bad behavior by complaining that he doesn't know better, be cautious. This game may work for him for a while until a pattern of behavior emerges. He can't "not know" forever. He could be stalling for time, searching for other ways of manipulating you into accepting his role as a "bad boy." Don't buy into it and don't let him make you act like his mother. This is your relationship, too and you're supposed to feel comfortable, safe and secure. Claiming ignorance doesn't excuse bad behavior when the behavior is repeated again and again. It's a form of passive aggression and a sign that this is a man who is just *too* wrong.

We have found that you can't change this type of man and you can't fix him. Chances are that he will continue bad behaviors with women, even when he's sixty. Bad behavior is bad behavior. Period. Stating clearly what you want and need, determining if he's willing and able and watching his actions (NOT his words) are the fastest and best way we know to see what kind of guy you've really got.

Just when I'd be ready to leave the relationship, he'd come through in some small way and convince me he was really changing. Then he'd be great, very sweet and loving—for a while. I wanted to believe that he was changing; he kept telling me he was. It was my friends who kept telling me what a manipulator he was and to open my eyes. It wasn't about his age...he knew what to do. That's just the kind of guy he was.

Lori (age 39)

When you witness or experience bad behavior from your younger man, try to step back emotionally and look at the events that have transpired. Is this a case of being too young or *too* wrong? Perhaps you're one of the first women to ever confront him about these things, because the women his age haven't had the courage to be straight with him. Or perhaps this is his nature and he doesn't care enough to be loving and kind. If so, then you are making excuses for him. Remember that every man's life is filled with a series of corrections, from the first female he encounters—his mother—to the last. Hopefully, he has listened and learned to be more sensitive, mannerly and giving. Once beyond his twenties, his behavior becomes more the product of his own determination. He should have been exposed to enough women by now to internalize and display acceptable behavior.

Observe his actions and decide for yourself what is going on with him. Once you've spoken your piece, give him some time to incorporate the information. Then check the willing and able criteria. Only then will you know if he's too young or just *too* wrong.

Chapter 9

Commitment: Can He or Can't He?

Every relationship ends. And usually one person leaves first, unless you both die in an accident together. We don't know what the future is going to be.
Kathryn Janus, psychotherapist

Cultural Perceptions

We saw a young woman on a television talk show express her disapproval of her fifty-something mother's relationship with a man of thirty-five. "I'm worried," said the daughter, in obviously heartfelt agony, "that he won't be able to make a real commitment to my mother." Of course, the mother and her younger man had, at the time of the airing of this show, already been happily married for five years and had lived together for several years before that. Still, despite the young man's having made what seems to us to be the ultimate commitment—marriage—the daughter was oblivious to the reality of her mother's situation. She was blinded by the assumption that simply because her mother's husband was younger he couldn't commit and, because her mother was older, he would eventually leave. Projecting her fears twenty-five years into the future, the worried daughter continued to question the man's willingness to "be there for her" when the mother was eighty and he only sixty. As though anyone, of any age, can predict what is going to happen to them twenty-five years in the future. Still, the daughter persisted and it became clear that no amount of logic was going to persuade her otherwise. How sad for this young woman, we thought, that she was so unable to share her mother's joy or be happy for her apparent contentment. How tragic that the daughter's unwillingness to accept her mother's husband was based not on some awful reality—that he was abusive, selfish or dishonest. No, she even acknowledged that he was none of these things. Her inability to accept this relationship was entirely based on a culturally imposed mythology. There sat the blissfully happy mom cuddled up with her adoring husband, while the poor, hand-wringing daughter bemoaned what she assumed to be her mother's fate twenty-five years hence. Something was, we thought, pathetically wrong with this picture.

Why are we so convinced that because a man is young he is commitment challenged? And why do we also automatically assume that women who choose younger men are somehow inherently defective, dysfunctional or at least avoiding commitment? Do we know these assumptions to be true? Or are they again false beliefs perpetuated by a society that can't or won't understand this kind of relationship?

Lynn Harris, a clinical social worker from Jamestown, New York comments:

> *Regarding young men and commitment, I think there is a prejudice and stereotype there and, like any other prejudice and stereotype, it's not accurate. In fact, it's insulting to young men; if I were a young man, I'd be offended.*
>
> *It assumes that they are psychologically impaired and emotionally crippled. Young men are committing to women all the time; they are, indeed, getting married. So why would it be viewed as anything different if the woman is older?*
>
> *Then, of course, there is an even lower form of stereotype, which is that older women are themselves so emotionally needy or desperate that they are therefore selecting men who can't commit. The whole assumption is ridiculous.*

What is the origin of these beliefs? Who perpetuates them? We believe the answer lies deeply embedded in the cultural perception of "youth and beauty." We have been told for centuries that a woman's worth and desirability reside in these qualities. We have also been the recipients of the message that a man can't possibly want or commit to a woman who is older than he, as these qualities (supposedly) diminish with age.

Feminist writer Naomi Wolf brilliantly exposes the origins of this belief system in her book, *The Beauty Myth* and reveals their socio-economic roots:

> *"Beauty" is a currency like the gold standard. Like any economy, it is determined by politics, and in the modern age in the West it is the last, best belief system that keeps male dominance intact.*

As a society, we have been both overtly and subliminally subjected to a steady barrage of this kind of psychological input. It is not surprising the worried daughter is so terrified about her mother's future. She doesn't understand how this man could be attracted to, and stay attracted to, a woman ten, fifteen or more years his senior. The daughter is more a victim of damaging cultural perceptions than a perpetrator intent upon destroying her mother's happiness.

Often, people without prior direct exposure to an older woman/younger man relationship automatically express dismay at this union. No one in their immediate circle has been involved in this type of thing. Therefore, they assume, it must be impossible. If they did have direct experience and exposure, they probably wouldn't rush to a negative conclusion, for such a mind-set is one born of ignorance, fear and discrimination.

The only exposure many people have had to older women/younger men couples has been through tabloid articles about famous movie stars or other celebrities. In many of these couplings, one person has so much more power and money than the other that, along with the very public nature of their lives and the pressure this imposes, a successful relationship with anyone, of any age, would be almost impossible to sustain. Yet when the relationship ends, blame is placed squarely on the age difference.

Those Who Commit

The experiences of friends and acquaintances as well as the hundreds of individuals who were interviewed for this book suggest a different reality. We've uncovered numerous stories of very much younger men who not only can and do commit to their older women, but take on the responsibility of a ready-made family as well.

Susan, a family friend, recently shared her cousin's story with us: Julie was thirty-five when she met Dan, age twenty. Julie's husband was abusive, violent and addicted to drugs and alcohol. They had five children ranging in age from eight to fifteen. The eldest boy was only a few years younger than Dan. Julie met Dan during the time she was separated from her husband and raising her children by herself. Dan pursued her. It was Julie who had a problem with the age difference, not Dan. He knew he wanted Julie and wasn't deterred by her age or the fact that she had five children from a previous marriage. It took him four years to convince her to marry him, because of her fears not his. She finally gave in, and Dan has since proved to be a wonderful husband and father. He has provided a sense of love and stability to Julie that her first (and older) husband could not. They have been happily married for six years now. We met this couple at a picnic and were struck by the love and mutual respect they radiated.

Carol, another friend of ours, told us about her sister, Jennifer, who had married Todd, a much younger man (seventeen years younger) almost twenty-five years ago. She, too, had several children from a previous marriage and had also been involved with an unloving, uncaring man close to her own age. Jennifer's younger man also pursued her. He was ready and able to commit. Again, it was the woman who had reservations. Given the social climate twenty-five years ago, this union was highly unusual. The couple suffered severe family censure. They moved to another state to distance themselves from their hostile families and have lived together happily since. Given the current divorce rate, a twenty-five-year marriage is a testament to two people who really want to be together against all odds.

When it's the right match, age is not an issue. Still, women are made to feel vulnerable to society's false perceptions. They are made to feel insecure about their beloveds' staying power, to question their own sanity for making this choice and forced to endure the social stigma that others attach to these relationships.

> *When we first got together, I had several people tell me it was a self-esteem issue...that I didn't believe in myself, didn't believe I deserved more. It was harder, yes, because of his age, but it didn't ring true as to what these people were saying. Then one lady, actually a casual acquaintance, said, "You must have really high self-esteem to do this...I just couldn't handle it."*
>
> *I thought about it. It did take more self-esteem to feel comfortable, confident and secure with a much younger man. Then I looked at the women who said I had low self-esteem. They were all with men who weren't young, attractive or exciting. They were the ones with low self-esteem. They had chosen men that, quite frankly, were so old and dissipated that they couldn't run away or leave them.*
>
> **Berta (age 58)**

Ignorance, myths and false beliefs make older women/younger men couples pay a high price for love, a price that's not exacted from couples in which the age difference is reversed.

Couples, in which the woman is older and the man younger, have been forced to defend their choices to family, friends and society as a whole. Many of them had to make geographic moves or carefully) decrease their social circles to include only those people with whom they can be themselves. A simple choice—made for love—somehow challenges the very core of what is considered right or appropriate.

> *I always heard growing up that older men were better husbands—they knew how to treat women, they would respect and appreciate them. So I married older men—twice. Both husbands cheated on me and then divorced me. When Barry came along and was so much younger, I thought he wasn't*

the one. He couldn't be. What did he know about how to treat a woman? How could he be ready to settle down and be serious? He was only twenty-five. I was older and I didn't think he'd know how to take care of me—he wouldn't have the money or the head for it. I was so wrong. Here he was, this young guy just starting out in business, and he was so mature and stable. He was really solid, but I didn't think he'd be the one who'd really come through for me. So I fought it in the beginning—a lot.

In thinking about all the older guys I dated after my divorces, I got the message that I would be worth more to them because I was younger. My mother was sixteen years younger than my father and he just thought he was so lucky to have her. He treated her like a queen. Barry treated me the same way. It took me a long time to really trust him, even though he did all the right things. Eventually, I did it. He's number three—and it's been seven years now.

Lauren (age 45)

Commitment is the desire to hold hands with someone as we each confront our own personal demons, to not run away from the image reflected back to us by our mate. The easy way to avoid personal responsibility for our growth is to change partners. By seeing ourselves in a shiny new mirror we hope to erase "the problem." But "the problem" is always within us.

Whatever our "hot" buttons are, they will be revealed in our intimate relationships. In a conscious and committed relationship, the couple is willing to look at their issues together and work on them. That's the miracle of commitment—a safe, loving, accepting place in which to grow and heal.

I much more enjoy a committed relationship both for the sexual and emotional component. I mean a sexual intrigue can be very erotic, but without the bonding of trust and emotional connection, it fails of its own accord. "The jewel of wisdom is purchased at infinite price"—a very wise old saying.

Nigel (age 37)

Traditionally, marriage has been viewed as the ultimate form of commitment. Commitment, however, is really a state of mind, surpassing any formalized structure or agreement. Although marriage is not the only acknowledgment of commitment, it is a pretty good one. Any long-term partnership, whether the couple lives together or not, can be a committed relationship. Commitment demands a vested interest in staying together and working things out. Commitment also means that a couple is clearly a couple.

The assumption that older women/younger men relationships are probably doomed to be short-lived sexual adventures does not take into account the whole picture. However, even we were amazed at the large numbers of healthy, viable, long-term commitments (marriages, living together and other arrangements) that had been entered into by older women and younger men and were thriving.

> *We dated for about six months and then broke up. I don't even remember why now. And then I married—the marriage was extremely short-lived—and when it broke up I called him. When he picked up the phone, he just said, "I knew you'd be back and that we would be together." Now, remember, he was still in his twenties.*
>
> *When we did get back together for the second time, he had changed and I had changed. I guess it was the time that we needed. We lived together for the next five years.*
>
> **Jean (age 51)**

> *When Michael came along, I was so shut down. I was like, okay, you show me, because I'm not going to believe it until I see it. He was practically textbook perfect and I thought, okay, at some point he's going to break down and run away like the other guys. But he didn't. It's been nine years. It still amazes me when I think about it. He was the last person I would have thought would be committed forever.*
>
> **Jacqui (age 49)**

Those Who Don't Commit

While it's clear that younger men can and do commit to older women, we wanted to examine the barriers that on occasion stand in the way of the men's commitment. Of the young men we spoke to, who were very much in love with their older women, less than 5 percent were unable to move into commitment. Why? We theorized before investigating that they were afraid the age difference would be more important with time or they wanted children or were fearful of losing their freedom or their identity, but discovered that there were other reasons.

> *It wasn't that I didn't want to be with Carolyn. She was great. I just didn't have the cash. I couldn't see how it could work—I mean, I really wanted to be with her, but I kind of looked like less next to her.*
>
> **Peter (age 31)**

> *There's a part of me that's still old-fashioned. I want to take care of my woman, wife, whatever. Or at least, to have it be fairly even. I couldn't really do that here. It was a lot of pressure. Not from her, mind you, it was me.*
>
> **James (age 33)**

It ended because I took a job in another state. I loved her, but I wanted
this job. It was the job or her.

Nick (age 35)

In these three cases, the men's inability to make commitments to the
women appeared at first to be about their lack of financial security. Some
of the young men we interviewed still held the traditional belief that they
should be able to take care of the woman financially, even though she had
an additional ten to twenty years of earning capacity. However, something
about this argument didn't ring true. The more we talked to men about
what had kept them from making commitments, the clearer it became that
it wasn't about finances at all.

My father told me there are two things you need to have in order for it
to be right—the right woman and the right time. She was definitely the right
woman, but it happened at the wrong time. I just couldn't see myself taking
a get-by job in order to do it. I had so much else I wanted to do. I wasn't ready
and I didn't want to make that kind of sacrifice.

Jeff (age 29)

As we listened more acutely, we began to realize that financial insecurity
was really just a convenient excuse. These were men who had narrowed
their choices to only two options—their romantic involvements vs. their
financial futures. Certainly there must have been other options but—in our
opinion—these were men who would be inclined to bail out anyway when
they hit bumps in the road. Finances proved to be a socially acceptable
bump. Realizing the women were special and worthy of more, their initial
fears allowed them to short-circuit the commitment. Not being financially
stable is a time-honored male excuse for backing out of a commitment (to
a woman of any age) and is widely accepted as an allowable out. While
there could have been another choice or a compromise, which is part and
parcel of commitment, these men chose to end the relationship.
Interestingly, each of these men is still single and still searching for that
"special someone."

Benefits of Commitment

Commitment in older women/younger men relationships can actually fos-
ter the motivation to advance. Almost 95 percent of the couples we interviewed talked about their search for economic balance and, for most, the
relationship proved to be a positive move on the younger man's part.

He turned his whole life around...he went from making a really low
income to making a really good income. He took a permanent job...and makes

pretty much what I make now. We bought a house together, planned and paid for our wedding...

Elaine (age 51)

Peter and June met when he was bouncing between odd jobs. He had never felt the motivation to focus on one career path, until he fell in love with June.

She had a lot to do with my going into pharmaceutical sales. I wanted to make it work for us and I think I was hesitant to do it on my own. I liked the freedom of not being tied into anything specific, but I really hated the fact that I was always hustling to make the rent and car payments. I think I finally just wanted to grow up. She didn't push or anything, but I just got tired of living hand to mouth. It had been okay for me, but would not be for us.

Peter (age 33)

Looking closer at the couple dynamics, we saw that at some point these young men made internal decisions—the women were worth it and they were ready to move to another level. Perhaps they decided to grow up or be responsible or to fully commit themselves to their relationship. Living just for themselves no longer worked. They were ready to share and ready for partnership.

I was kind of stuck. I'd been cruising along. I didn't really think much about it at the time. It's like I couldn't keep doing it the way I was doing it. It just didn't work anymore. Kelly was always a go-getter. She loved her job and she was so enthusiastic. I couldn't understand it at first. But she was really psyched about her career and I think it rubbed off on me.

Martin (age 28)

Jean and Michael relayed their story to us. They initially lived together for five years and then married eleven years ago. Jean is now fifty-one, and Michael is forty. Jean told us:

Michael decided to go back to school when I met him—he's a physicist now. He figured if something was going to happen between the two of us, he would have to go back and finish up his college. It was about us being in the same world.

Jean went on to explain that Michael's decision was based upon wanting to increase his income in order to be with her and she was already highly successful in her own business. Not only has Michael since earned quite a handsome living, but his family credits Jean directly for his success. They see the big picture. Michael's desire to be equally matched financially prompted him to renew an old interest in physics and to develop himself fully in that area. With so many of the couples we spoke to, the relationship with an older woman provided the motivation for the younger man to achieve more and accomplish more in order to be on a par with his mate. In these instances, it was the older woman who served as a catalyst in helping the younger man to not only set but achieve higher goals.

Another reason some men are unable to commit has to do with developmental issues. Regardless of age, a man must have completed the stages of individuation and established his own identity. This process requires work and maturation and isn't contingent upon one's chronological age. If a man hasn't experienced healthy bonding within his family of origin, he will probably express this in a relationship. He may cling too closely to his mate and become overly dependent. He may reject closeness out of his fear of being engulfed by the woman and losing his identity. If he hasn't separated from his parents, a woman would do well to walk, if not run, from this type of young man.

The classic case of a man with commitment problems is one that most women have encountered at some point in their lives. It looks like this: He aggressively pursues her, convinces her that he's available and willing to make a commitment. Then, as soon as she lets go emotionally and gets involved, he runs away. His longing for connection battles with his fear of connection, and in the ensuing chaos he withdraws from the relationship.

When a man (of any age) says to you that he needs "space," watch out! You're in for a rough ride. He is in conflict about partnership. To him, commitment equals loss of self. Somewhere in his family of origin, being close has probably meant giving up his personal needs and desires.

> This whole "space" thing with guys drives me totally nuts. If I hear one more guy tell me he needs his space, I'm really going to smack him. What is it about the "space" thing? They come after you—so hard—they convince you they want a relationship, then you finally let go and trust them and they pull this "space" nonsense. I've really had it. As far as I'm concerned, you can keep all of them. They're not worth it. I think I'm going to marry my girl-friend—really—she cooks, keeps house—really. I think it's a better deal.
>
> **Anna (age 42)**

> At first I thought it was due to age. He'd come close, then back off. It wasn't until I saw that he treated his friends and his family the same way—very intense beginnings, then violent endings—that I finally got it. Everyone got the same treatment from him. Everyone was called a manipulator by him. Everyone got left—suddenly and dramatically.
>
> **Vicky (age 48)**

Sadly, it seems as though society encourages this type of behavior in which men pursue women, then back off when commitment appears imminent. It's the classic playboy model and sowing-wild-oats excuse and such behavior leaves the emotional wreckage of confused and hurt women in its wake. It is perceived as a male prerogative—love them and leave them and don't suffer any consequences. You may try to rationalize his behavior—perhaps he was engulfed by his mother, his father was emotionally unavailable, he was never breast-fed. The bottom line, however, is that he can't commit and you've got a problem.

Fortunately, many young men are ready to commit, regardless of age. Approximately 10 percent of the multitude of couples in our study became seriously involved when the men were in their early twenties. Although this isn't necessarily the norm, it can and does happen. Many men are stable and mature at a young age. We've also seen younger men make the leap into maturity propelled by their love for older women. Many of these men told us that the relationships themselves helped them to grow up. Being with older women provided the support for their growth and commitment. Because of the women's solidity and maturity, the men could achieve a type of partnership not possible with younger women who were still trying to find themselves.

For a young man standing on the precipice of commitment, the view can be daunting. He has one foot in the world of his peers and one foot in your world. The motivation to make the leap is fueled by the intensity of his love for and desire to be with you. His friends may be living a different lifestyle. He wants to be his age, but he also wants to be with you. A young man may be torn in different directions, going against what is "normal," jumping out of his developmental sequence and merging with your world. Whether commitment to you means an agreement to see each other exclusively, live together or be married, he is forced to make a choice in order to keep you. This is a great and courageous leap and it is one for which men are not highly rewarded. Our society offers little or no support for the personal evolution of men. They get credit for their achievements in the world, their ability to make money and to be leaders. Little credit is given to men for being devoted mates or loving parents.

The Emerging Commitment Model

While men have certainly been making commitments to women for longer than we can remember, the old commitment archetype embodied some different qualities and attributes. Usually, men weren't the ones who had to sacrifice anything in order to be in a committed relationship. In the generations prior to the women's movement of the 1960s, commitment usually meant marriage and marriage generally meant that the men worked outside of the home and had opportunities to achieve success and satisfaction in the world. The women usually lived in the communities in which their husbands had to live because of career requirements. Women had to sacrifice their dreams and aspirations in order to live up to their part of the commitment bargain—raising the children. This is old news. So is what often happens to women even today who don't live up to their husbands' or partners' checklists of ways to meet their needs. Frequently, if the women are over forty, they get replaced, especially if they try to evolve toward achieving some satisfaction in their own right.

When a younger man commits to an older woman, he is often the one who chooses to make some sacrifices in order to perpetuate the relationship. This is something new and worthy, we think, of recognition. A young man who takes on the responsibility of the woman's children, who endures social and familial censure, who willingly pairs himself with a woman who, more often than not, has already achieved a position of power in the world and isn't going to be obedient out of fear of losing him, is an evolved creature. He chooses to endure these obstacles because he loves and wants to be with the woman, because he values the partnership and because he understands the healing properties of true commitment. Having been raised in an era in which women were more able to self-actualize, men in their twenties and thirties are used to dealing with women as equals and are able to do so far more comfortably than men in their forties and beyond. The commitment model becomes inherently more evolved than its predecessors. We think this is good news for everyone.

Long Unions

At this period in history, when serial monogamy and a high divorce rate seem to be the norm for many couples, we wondered about the nature of long unions. What is the secret that eludes so many of us? Is it, as disk jockey Wolfman Jack once said, "Love is not a matter of counting the years—it's making the years count"? We asked Dr. Marcella Bakur Weiner, clinical psychologist, author of *Stalemates: The Truth About Extramarital Affairs* and professor of psychology at Marymount Manhattan College in New York City. Here are some of her thoughts on the subject:

> *How can some couples stay together for twenty, thirty or more years? Or even five or ten years? What makes it work? For one, the expectation that we can really totally change the other person no longer exists, if it ever did. Think about it. As each of us grows older, starting from birth, we become more and more of who we are and who we were meant to be. No two babies are exactly alike; one is quiet—the other more active; one is verbally articulate—the other more retreating. These are qualities that will stay around for all of life. If that person is unhappy with that trait, they will look to change it. But no one else can do it. In long-term relationships, there is not only an*

allowance for each partner to be himself or herself, but, more than that, there is encouragement. The understanding is: "You are who you are and I love you for it, and I am who I am and I know you feel the same." While affirming their couple status, the two people recognize the need to be authentically themselves. No one is a slave or glued to the other.

Long-term unions also have to do with the lack of fear. Fear of what? It could be anything, but is usually wrapped in the "What if?" syndrome. It goes something like this: "Yes, I think it's all very good right now. But...what if...tomorrow I/she/he will lose a job; hate each other; disagree on some major issues; find someone we like better; get old and have to take care of each other?—and on and on and on. Instead of concentrating on the here and now, the beauty of the moment and just living and loving, the anxiety is projected into the future with a million possibilities none of which, most likely, will ever happen. But it takes time and energy for all these worries to get going and little is left over for just staying in the present and tasting/feeling the fullness of life. People who remain in long-term relationships have freed themselves from these "What if?" tormenting demons. Avoiding these demons can be a major challenge for older women/younger men couples. For here again, based upon the myths of aging with which we in the western world are plagued, the "What ifs?" turn into: "And when I'm eighty and you're sixty, will you still love me?" The reverse is also possible: "When I'm sixty and you're eighty, will we still have something in common and will I still care?" Commitment, however, is commitment.

If the older woman/younger man couple is going to make it, they have a good head start, because they have already broken the ice and gone against mainstream society. They have put their energies, ideas, feelings and love into their relationship. If doubt begins to creep in and the demons poke their little forks at you, you can just toss them off by thinking of all the many reasons you chose this particular partner and how perfect the match is for you. What is little known in modern society is that, according to all research on aging, the least viable factor of importance is the actual age of the person. What is the most relevant to age, per se, is not the date on your birth certificate, but how you feel. Yes, not even how you look is as important.

A good exercise, a visualization to do if and when you are feeling testy about longtime unions and remaining committed, is to imagine yourself without your partner. Closing your eyes, get into your emotions and feel fully your inner experience. See yourself alone. Now, see yourself together with the other person. Feel their presence, smell their scent, touch their skin (with eyes still closed) and feel what sensations come to you. Open your eyes and be aware of the experience. Then ask your partner to do the same and reaffirm, to each other, your long-term commitment. Finish off with a toast—to a love forever and more.

Chapter 10

Power

I didn't want to date younger men, but men my age and older tell me I'm intimidating. Younger guys say they're "turned on" by what they perceive as my power and accomplishments while older men reject all that I've become.
Barbara (age 44)

Money and power in exchange for youth and beauty—the traditional form of barter in our patriarchal society has been based upon this formula. Older men "buy" the youth and beauty of younger women and supply them with money and power. Marriage based upon this unspoken agreement has long been some women's easiest way to increase their economic and social status. Is this a fair trade? A more germane question is, considering today's shifting dynamics with women working and developing their own power base, is it a worthwhile trade? More and more women think not. Yet there are also some women who still choose to enter relationships which play out this old archetype. They believe that they will benefit. But do they really?

When one person is viewed as the "have" and the other the "have not," there is inherent potential for some serious resentment on both sides. In sharing his status and money, the man of means (the "have") expects certain functions from his ("have not") wife. After all, if he's buying her, he should get his money's worth.

> *In my opinion, the woman is selling her sexual favor in exchange for luxury, safety and security. She thinks she'll get the freedom and leisure to not have to worry about her own existence. But it's not an equal relationship.*

As a man playing this game, it's totally dissatisfying. You're never really loved...in the end you're respected for being a good provider. The relationship is not set up to be about love. As soon as he marries her, she complains he's too controlling. As far as the man is concerned, he's paying through the nose for it. We are deeply embedded in sexist role-playing that is deadly to both genders.

John (age 60)

The wife's primary purpose in this type of relationship is to fulfill her husband's needs and support his lifestyle—whether that means relocating for his business, giving up a career or working in a limited way that allows her to be available to him. Because he is paying and therefore in control, she is subjugated to his choices. If she is non-compliant or seeks too much of a life of her own, there is frequently a rift. She runs the risk (often unknowingly) of being replaced by another woman who can provide youth and beauty, but with fewer personal requirements. Some young women are, of course, quite content with this arrangement.

Look at everything I've got. I really don't mind having sex with him. He doesn't even want it all that often.

Alice (age 26) married to Norm (age 59)

The women who enter these types of relationships often find themselves contained within clearly defined boxes. Certainly they can evolve, but not so much as to threaten the power the men have over them. They can work, but not to the point that it distracts them from meeting the men's needs. This point of view was succinctly stated by actor John Wayne, who once said, "They have a right to work wherever they want to—as long as they have dinner ready when you get home."

If a woman involved in such a union makes the "mistake" of growing outside of her imposed boundaries, she tips the scales of the power structure. Being more, wanting more, doing more is a threat to the man and the relationship. If she grows beyond these boundaries, the reason to keep her (pay for her, support her) is destroyed. In the eyes of many men who have made this kind of bargain, replacement is necessary.

We were married for twenty-seven years and, I thought, very happily. He was a psychiatrist and we had a wonderful life, three beautiful children and a great relationship. When the children left home, I decided to go back to school for my Ph.D. I was busy and excited about what I was doing so when he told me he wanted a divorce, I was stunned. I didn't even know that anything had been wrong! I was shocked beyond belief. He moved out the same night and he wouldn't even talk to me. I found out later, through the children, what had been the basis of his rage at me. Since I went back to school there were three nights a week that I wasn't home to have his dinner on the table. After twenty-seven years, that's what was intolerable to him. He remarried within a year of the divorce.

Marianna (age 62)

When we look at the long-term marriages that have dissolved because of the woman's need to grow, we also note the choice of mate the man often seeks for comfort—a less empowered woman. One with fewer needs, wants and ambitions. Most women over the age of forty can cite numerous stories of women—public and private—who grew into their own power only to be replaced by a woman (usually younger) with none. Do the names Ivana and Marla ring any bells?

The struggle for power and control rears its ugly head in various ways among couples locked into this old pattern. As women mature, they are called into the fullness of their being. They instinctively seek to become whole and complete, which can threaten the male power base. When forced to relinquish all power, many women resort to more underhanded means of re-establishing it. Control and manipulation become the weapons of choice. Regaining control through spending his money wildly is a legendary payback for the resentment of being the "have not."

Betty Friedan wrote in her classic book, *The Feminine Mystique*, that "it is easier to live through someone else than to become complete yourself." We have learned that it just looks easier—at least for a while—until the internal mechanism that forces us to evolve into our own identity becomes impossible to repress. Fortunately, more and more women today are searching for ways in which they can fully develop their own powers within relationships based on true equality and partnership.

When confronted with an older woman/younger man couple, the automatic assumption by most people is that she is the one in control, that she is the one with all the power. They presume it's just a reversal of the traditional model between older men and younger women. But this is hardly the case. On the contrary, the typical power structure within an older woman/younger man relationship is so well balanced it could serve as a role model for younger couples seeking this kind of equilibrium.

When you are involved with an older woman, the competitive factor is removed. Especially if she's achieved a certain level of success—you're not competing with her from a career perspective.

Say a man is twenty-six and meets a girl twenty-four. In today's world, they are competing for the same career opportunities. I mean, thirty or forty years ago, the girl would be the nurse or the receptionist, and he would be the doctor. Now, they are both competing to be the cardiologist.

For me, I find I don't need the woman to subordinate herself to me and I don't need to be the breadwinner. You leapfrog all that into a more advanced relationship.

Nigel (age 37)

With the competition factor eliminated, and without the prescribed role of provider, the younger men we spoke to felt a greater sense of personal freedom and joy in these relationships. Having bypassed the expectations of a more traditional structure, they are there because they want to be, accepted for whom they are and free to achieve at their own pace.

Men have, after all, been programmed to create their own power and independence from birth. They have been encouraged to rise to their own level without the aid of a mate. It is almost impossible, even today, to equate a young man's power with a young woman's power. Historically, men haven't required protection, financial support or the help of a woman in order to advance their social status. Men of all ages have been socialized to stand on their own two feet. In serious relationships with women, most young men don't look to them to do it for them. Being men, they do what they've been taught to do—they enter the relationship with whatever power they possess and continue to develop their resources on their own.

The idea of the older woman being the "mommy" is really a paradoxical fiction. Because she is older, the woman is automatically perceived as the "mommy" in relationship to the younger man. But the definition of a "mommy" infers self-sacrifice and the giving up of one's own needs in order to tend to another's. The "mommy" is focused on providing care, nurturing and support. Actually, it is more often the unempowered younger woman, who gives up her dreams and career aspirations (her power) to be available to her older mate, who is closer to acting out the stereotypical "mommy" role. Her needs become secondary to those of her husband, her goals perceived as not as important as her mate's and her position frequently remains static.

This is the old archetype, one that many women who are today in their forties, fifties and sixties lived out when they were young women entering their first relationships. Ultimately, many of these relationships failed. The men weren't monsters or abusers. Most of them didn't consciously set out to repress their mates. It was just built into the nature of the relationship model. When the instinct to grow became overpowering, the women had to leave. Dr. Kathleen Calabrese comments:

Divorce statistics indicate that a significantly greater number of women than men initiate the dissolution of a long-term marriage. These

women leave their marriages because they feel terribly lonely, empty, unap-
preciated and undervalued by their husbands, not because they are being
beaten or because of affairs. Women are beginning to say yes to themselves
in spite of the extraordinary familial and cultural pressure to stay put, to
"know your place," and practice gratitude.

In some ways, traditional relationships are easy, because the roles are so
clearly defined that one finds in them comfort and security. In other ways—
say those who have escaped from them—they are impossible, because those
roles are so rigid and inflexible. One thing seems certain—"one up-one
down" relationships create hostility and resentment for both parties. Finding
ourselves locked in narrow and stifling roles, our interior selves fight for freedom. Frequently, the "one up" player resents the "one down" if the expectations of need aren't fulfilled. The one in control may seek to diminish the
other. The "one down" resents the "one up" for being forced to endure powerlessness and will overtly or covertly seek revenge. Control, manipulation,
games and power struggles ensue. It is an unhealthy relationship dynamic.

Having experienced the old archetype from the man's perspective, we
appreciated the candor displayed by our friend John, age sixty, when he
discussed the high price that men also pay for this model:

> *The old paradigm is based on co-dependency. I'm the success object and*
> *she's the sex object. I don't want to "buy" my love and play out the traditional*
> *dysfunction.*
>
> *I don't see a lot of men out there who are saying, "I'm very happy by*
> *myself and I seek even greater fulfillment within myself." My friends that*
> *have money and power and so on...If I was sitting in a room with ten of these*
> *guys, and a beautiful woman came in, the other guys would throw in every-*
> *thing that they have to possess her...houses, airplanes, promises, money,*
> *whatever. I don't want to compete in this game.*
>
> *I had to learn to develop and give myself all the aspects a man tradi-*
> *tionally gets from a woman...and women have to learn how to become self-suf-*
> *ficient in their maleness. Once that's in place, she has a choice as to the type*
> *of relationship she wants to be in. If she's independent and has her own auton-*
> *omy, would she then want to marry an old man simply because he has money?*

When we eliminate need, we get choice. When we both come from the
power of choice, we have the opportunity to experience equality. No longer
based on two incomplete people seeking to be completed, the emerging older
women/younger men relationships we're seeing more often illustrate the
ideal of two complete people who simply want to be together.

The illusion of control also created the illusion of safety in many traditional relationships. But, alas, as with all illusions, the harsh light of reality

beams through at some point. It is a recognized spiritual paradox that what is small is really large and what appears to loom largest is actually very small. Real strength doesn't need to exert itself. Real wealth doesn't need to be flaunted. Real power is internal and doesn't need to project itself as power over others.

But how can a savvy woman tell what a man really wants? How can she read between the lines and discern the true subtext of what he says? How will she know what type or extent of control—or lack thereof—a man really seeks? All of us—even the most evolved and aware older women (and men)—have our agendas. It's just that as we become more conscious and evolved we are able to admit to them. Many older men who have not worked on their personal growth cannot express or honestly face their true agendas. We have developed a tip sheet to help you translate their language. Our own massive research on what some men say and what they really mean has brought us to these conclusions:

When an older man says:	What he means is:
"I don't mind if a woman works, but not too much."	She's got to have an unimportant job she can leave at any moment to take care of *my* needs. I must be the total focus of her life.
"I know a lot of single older women in their forties and fifties—they're very successful, but they're not feminine."	I feel insecure around a woman who thinks for herself. She may challenge me. My insecure older friends are also threatened by female power.
"A woman can know who she is, but shouldn't be too headstrong. I find it utterly unattractive."	I want someone without an established identity that I can control. I don't want to be challenged or be responsible for my actions.
"I don't want to work again when I go home."	I want an unevolved beauty with few personal needs. I don't want her to have a lot of ambition other than being totally there for me. If she is too smart or independent, she may call me on my deficiencies and I'll have to look at myself.
"She's got to have at least one body part that's outrageous—great legs, a terrific ass, something...I need to feel sexually attracted to her."	Even though my skin is saggy, my stomach huge and there's more hair on my back than on my head, *she* needs to be beautiful and well preserved. After all, I'm a man, and I'm historically entitled to youth and beauty, even though I have neither.
"I'm meeting lovely older women, but I just don't feel chemistry for them."	To hell with inner worth—I want red hot sex. I want a wild tiger in bed, who's young, firm and emotionally undemanding. I just don't have enough money to attract one, so I'm stuck on blind dates with age appropriate women.

These, then, are the types of comments that an older man might make to conceal how totally intimidated he is by an evolved and independent older woman. Barbara, a successful forty-four-year-old, was confused:

> *I didn't want to date younger men, but men my age and older tell me I'm intimidating. Yes, I've done a lot with my life...I thought that was the point! I'm financially secure, world traveled and I know I look great. But older men reject all that I've become, while the younger guys say they're "turned on" by what they perceive as my power and accomplishments. What's the deal?*

Good question. We too wanted to know why it is that at one point a woman's strengths are considered assets—then become liabilities depending on the man's age. *Why are young guys intrigued by her and so many older men intimidated by her?* We asked the men this question. We appreciated their honesty with us. Once again, the issue boiled down to power and control. As men get older they feel a tremendous loss of what they no longer have. They aren't as strong physically as they once were. They don't have the energy and drive they once possessed and in many ways feel their power slipping away. In order to feel good about themselves, they prefer to be with someone who makes them feel stronger by comparison.

A great many women have traditionally perceived their men as having both strengths and weaknesses and have loved them for both characteristics. We wondered why many older men couldn't accept and love the strengths of older women as well as their weaknesses. Why not allow each person to own their strengths—why the conflict?

> *It's because we develop these fears, these voices in our heads that say,* You could have done more, maybe you didn't do enough, make enough, achieve enough, and now it's too late.
>
> **Carl (age 59)**

> *I'm the only one of my male friends who thinks like this—I want equality in a male/female relationship. But even I start to wonder if I'm enough for her if she's really powerful. Will she want me, need me? You see, it's about fear really. We feel safe if we have control—and I mean total control. Men can't separate "this" control from "that" control. It's an all or nothing issue.*
>
> **Bill (age 62)**

It seems total control equals total security for many men. Security means that a man is needed. If the woman is incomplete, less experienced than the man and needy, he can feel safe. Okay, this is not so hard to understand. It even—sadly—makes a certain amount of sense. But why don't younger men seem to worry about their safety and security when they are involved with older women, especially given the often glaring power differences?

She has power and that's sexy. I'm not thinking that because she has power it means I can't have power. It's like I'm really powerful to even have her love me. But it's great to be with a woman who's got a lot to offer. I can learn. It's exciting.

Anthony (age 25)

I'm not into competing with women. I don't get it with men and women competing. We are different and sometimes we are in different places in our lives. As long as there is the attraction, and it works, I don't care how much power she has. You know, it's funny, because I know guys who have to have all the control and be on top. But they're the guys who really aren't sure of themselves. It shouldn't be that I'm more so you are less.

Carlos (age 37)

As an artist, having money, success and power was never uppermost in my mind. Leslie definitely was a very successful woman when we met. I couldn't have competed if I wanted to—she was making a lot of money then and that was ten years ago. She's even more successful now.

Because she dealt with it very well, and we dealt with it together, she never rubbed it in my face. It was never a power struggle as to who was paying for what. Frankly, I held my ground; I had my own money. Anyway, she could have bought and sold me ten times, but we just didn't let those issues infringe on our relationship.

It's very interesting for a young man to be the one who brings the "grounding" into a relationship. Her life is very fast paced and I know I ground her.

Lenny (age 38)

Maybe the correlation has to do with the fact that a young man who is willing to become involved (remember, we're talking about long-term relationships here) with an older woman is an individual who already has enough personal power and security to risk it in the first place. Maybe, as psychotherapist Kathryn Janus points out, younger men have been raised differently:

My husband is much more of a feminist than I. He will point out something to me in a movie or a television program that we're watching and he'll say, "That's so offensive to women," and I haven't been offended—but he's been offended! Younger men have grown up with the women's movement—

and I had to make that transition. I have an "old" way of seeing women sometimes...I don't even realize it, but my husband will point it out to me.

Whatever the reasons are, the point to remember is that, despite the most popular misconceptions and attitudes, surprisingly large numbers of older women/younger men relationships work—and work well—and do so on many different levels. And while the dominant power structure, the one created by men and maintained by the current older male population, tries to devalue and de-sexualize older women, how good it is to realize that where the old model falls away, a far more woman-friendly model is emerging in its place.

Chapter 11

Equality

When I moved into my boyfriend's apartment (we married a year later), he generously emptied out two whole dresser drawers for me to keep my things in. I was so touched. I thought we were really "sharing." Who knew?
Maya (age 50)

Equality

In light of the vast socio-economic shifts of the last half century, most women today realize they cannot duplicate the types of relationships their mothers and grandmothers experienced. Far too much water has passed under the bridge of change.

Reflecting upon the old marital archetype, which was a barter system, we realized that a number of our female forerunners benefited from this type of power alliance. Many women experienced the best of the historic archetype. They married successful, devoted and respectful men who gladly shared their money, position and status with their wives. They were loved by their husbands and led lives of varying degrees of luxury and comfort. Indeed, by society's standards, these women "did well."

Not every woman benefited from the old model, however. The same system that offered a life of ease and comfort to many women also had a darker side for many others. Several of the women we interviewed recall their mothers secretly pilfering the allotted grocery money and hiding it from their husbands in order to buy something for the children. At least 35 percent of the women we interviewed have vivid memories of verbal and physical abuse and of witnessing the unhappiness their mothers suffered due to their entrapment in an environment from which they could not escape.

These women were also financially dependent upon their husbands, but their husbands' lack of authentic power, sensitivity and generosity created a system of female servitude, indebtedness and powerlessness. Many of these women sacrificed their happiness and quietly accepted the prescribed roles. The quality of their lives was compromised by the same system that offered others great contentment and well-being.

While we might look at our mothers and envy some of the elements they shared with their husbands in the traditional marital archetype, most of us would, or have had to, make our own changes to those prescribed roles. Today, we are not comfortable repeating by rote our mates' political and social views. Rather, we may differ strongly from their perspectives. Neither do we feel comfortable living in their shadow. Most of the women we know enjoy healthy levels of autonomy in their personal lives and rewarding self-expression in their work. At the dawn of the twenty-first century, the idea of giving up a career for a man or even relocating at his company's whim is perceived as unfair, if not oppressive.

While we definitely have a desire to alter the existing marital or relationship roles of men and women, many of us like certain aspects of the old form. However, each woman is so vastly different in her needs that it is no wonder the men out there are confused. While one woman may need to be pampered and fussed over, another may need quiet, quality time alone. We've heard such a range of descriptions regarding what a man "should be" and what a man "should do" that in the end, each woman must be very clear about what she wants and needs and effectively communicate that to her mate.

The new model has no former model to draw from. We hear women repeatedly say, "I want the man to be the man." But what exactly does that mean nowadays? In former times, the roles were very clearly defined for each gender. The concept of equality didn't factor into the equation. There was no equality, but there was a clear trade-off: "I'll give you this, if you give me that." It was a barter system at best. Problems arose when one partner did not fulfill the expectations of his or her role or pressed to renegotiate what was a real but unspoken agreement.

Now the lines are blurred and the expectations much more individualized. While we still see examples of men giving up their Saturdays, patiently (or impatiently) waiting for their wives to finish shopping so they may perform their husbandly duty and pay the bill, the reality is that the traditional archetype is an old form that is dying. We now wonder how many Gen-X and Gen-Y girls actually expect to be supported financially. Is it a fairy tale they heard that happened a long time ago?

Today, more and more women have money, power, status and their own sense of independence and freedom. We no longer need to be dependent upon a man for our survival needs. Our newfound identities as complete beings marks the end of a cycle of powerlessness and binding our fate to that of another. However, in the act of embracing personal power, we are subject to many new choices. The dynamic that formed the glue of the old model has been torn apart. With the added dimension of two individuals seeking union in the new prototype, the options and choices can be over-whelming. What does this new equality look like? How do we create a model that works for us and our partners as well? What role do men take now? How do women combine careers and family while formulating the connective bond with their partners?

The older women and younger men we interviewed have created new and viable models of equality. They have held onto their own identities, their own finances and have still been able to share in committed and lov-ing partnerships. Each couple has carved out their own version of what the man does and what the woman does. One thread, however, is consistent throughout—these women all feel loved and valued.

Gail, age fifty-one, works as a hair stylist. About ten years ago, she met Lou at a friend's party. Gail had been worried about being single in her for-ties—she didn't like to party, didn't enjoy the bar scene and rarely went out. Although her friends constantly urged her to get out of the house, as Gail explained to us, she was exhausted when she came home from work:

> *I stand on my feet all day and all I do is talk to people and interact with them. The last thing I want to do when I get home is get dressed up and go out again. My friends told me I would never meet anyone and I knew, on some level, they were right. But the whole scene was just too much pres-sure...to be on, to be interesting.*

Gail told us that she met Lou on one of those rare nights when she made herself go out, mostly because it was her dear friend's birthday party. She and Lou were both sitting alone in a corner of the room. He didn't really care to mingle either, but knew the husband of the birthday girl from work. As they chatted, they discovered they had a lot in common. Both loved to be at home, loved to read and watch movies and videos. They appreciated a quiet night at home. Gail remembered laughing and telling Lou that "they would be a perfect couple."

Lou worked in sales and was often on the road. At thirty, he had a major territory to cover and spent hours with clients and prospective clients. For Lou, sales was a seven-day-a-week job, with many weekend hours spent on the phone checking and placing orders. Gail explained:

> *I could see he was younger than I, but we were in the same place in life. We enjoyed talking with each other that night and I gave him my number. At first we treated our relationship as "just friends." We talked about work and*

our lives in a general way. Then one night I asked him if he wanted to come over, since I had rented a really great movie. That was it. We became a regular item. We could both relax with each other. No pressure. No games.

Being reclusive at heart, Gail had met her perfect match in quiet Lou. While they both work and enjoy their jobs, their dispositions are well suited and their eleven-year age difference doesn't pose any problems. They are in the same place in life and enjoy a ten-year marriage of warmth and commitment. Gail glowed when she spoke about their union:

Yes, I do feel adored and I feel I can be me. On our days off we both like to sleep in and then enjoy breakfast together and read. We are hermits, I guess. But since so much of our work life demands that we be active and involved with people, it is great just to be with someone who is easy.

This is one of the new models of relationship equality: Two people who share their leisure time and enjoy each other's company, who work, maintain separate checking accounts, separate investments and split the rent and bills at the end of each month. Gail and Lou share the cooking responsibilities according to who is working late that night. Each does his or her own laundry and they trade off weeks on who picks up (and pays for) the groceries.

Today's relationships cover a wide expanse of lifestyles, interests and behavioral codes. As women actively choose which portions of the traditional relationship menu they want to retain, they are also asking for more "a-la-carte" items. Many have made up an entirely new menu. The roles of men and women in partnership have vastly different components now and the good news is the freedom we have in choosing what works for us, rather than squeezing ourselves into the traditional model. With this new freedom, however, comes the need for negotiation and clear knowledge of oneself.

We met Louise, age thirty-two, at a conference. Although we didn't intend to interview her at the time (since she was not actively involved with a younger man), she did shed light on what her thirty-something group is experiencing in today's world.

Louise told us she had dated younger men, as well as much older men, and specifically had problems meeting available men in her own age group. Her female friends and co-workers were also in a similar position. Louise works for a major accounting firm and has a very high-powered job. She spends most of her time outside the office in work-related relationships and spends the early evening hours at the office, on her computer or at business dinners. Her weekends are spent on airplanes traveling to meetings in other cities. Her reading material consists of business reports and journals and she has not "read a book for pleasure" in years. Louise has no social life outside of her work. Like so many of today's working women who are actively supporting themselves and building a career, her opportunity to meet and mingle with available men is a luxury of a past era. While both she and her thirty-something friends would love to have committed, loving partnerships, they find it difficult to give up what they have worked so hard to attain in order to have the time and energy for a relationship. In their world, they are similar to men of the last century as well as many men of this era. Work comes first and if the opportunity arises for someone to fit into his or her life as it is, then they will consider a relationship.

What happens now that some women have the same emphasis on work and career that many men have? While it may represent equality in the work ethos of men and women, which partner in a relationship should be required to "give up" what he or she has? Traditionally, in the old archetype, a woman automatically "gave up" her career, abandoned her lifestyle and fit herself into the existing lifestyle of a man. Today, a woman's desire for partnership, the right kind of partnership, still exists, but she is unwilling to give up such a vital part of herself to get it. However, as Louise explained, men are also often unwilling to "give up" their careers:

We talk about this at work all the time. My friends all have great jobs and make great money. We have worked hard to get where we are and we work harder still to maintain it. Can you imagine asking a man to give up his job (and career) in order to be with us? It wouldn't happen. Men wouldn't think of doing it. As a matter of fact, my friend just got transferred to our London office, and her boyfriend basically said, "Too bad." There was no negotiation. I mean, it wasn't even up for discussion.

We asked Louise, if given these parameters of "your career vs. mine," could she possibly envision a type of man who would be willing to negotiate? She jumped in immediately:

Definitely a younger guy. Forget asking a fifty-year-old executive...they would have a coronary on the spot. No, definitely a guy who is younger, because they have grown up seeing women work and they are much more willing to share. It's just the way it is for them. All the young women we know are very focused on making lives for themselves. They aren't waiting around for men to do it for them—and the young men they date know that. These young men realize it is a dual work life and they know that's one of the things they'll have to deal with whenever they are with someone. It's normal for them.

Louise went on to explain that she has dated younger men, and although she enjoys the stability and worldliness of older men, she sees the trade-off as being one of more freedom and flexibility. While the older man has had more time to establish himself in his career and in the ways of the world, Louise told us that she, like her girlfriends, finds it difficult to deal with the older man in a relationship, primarily because of the expected deference to his taste, his identity and his lifestyle:

> *They (older men) expect you to come to them...to fit into their lives. It's like they have the whole thing worked out for themselves, and if you can fit in, fine. But forget asking them to reverse it. I dated an older man for about six months and everything was on his timetable, his schedule and had to do with his convenience. He was a great guy, very sweet, but just couldn't understand why I wouldn't see him on certain nights or just take off for a weekend and drop everything. You see, he expected it. He wasn't mean about it, but he was just confused. It's like it didn't compute for him. I'm the woman so I should give up whatever in order to be with him. Also, he never took my work seriously. There was an underlying idea that I was only temporarily working—that one day I would stop and then be ready for a relationship.*

In a partnership of equality, both individuals have their own lives and their own identities. One is not expected to give up one's life for the other's convenience. Today's woman knows that and holds onto what she has created for herself, even if that means she is alone. The thought of sacrificing her own goals, in order to be with a man, is absurd to her. She looks for a partnership in which she can be herself, sharing all of what she is and who she is with her mate, and together finding the balance in the relationship that works for both of them.

Work and Children

The arrival of children into a relationship many times further contributed to the calcification of male and female roles in the old model. Since a man could almost always earn a great deal more money than a woman, it made sense that he went out to work while she stayed home, raised the kids, cleaned the house and had dinner ready when he returned. Times have changed dramatically, however, and as more and more women have developed professional lives, responsibilities and success, the traditional system has been thrown into chaos. Younger men, many of whom have been raised with a feminist consciousness, are far more open and willing to share what had, in the past, been "women's work." Even so, today's younger women who have children as well as careers often complain that their mates' "help" around the house is still an unequal structure. Helping the person who is primarily responsible is not quite the same as "sharing" that responsibility. Even today's younger couples are struggling to define equality. The need to build a career *and* raise a child *and* fulfill the responsibilities of a relationship have made everyone struggle with the nature of equality in a partnership. It's a tough dilemma, to be sure.

The struggle eases up considerably, however, when the woman has been able to put her child-rearing duties mostly behind her and has reached a comfort level in her career. Over 80 percent of the women in our research were at such a juncture in their lives when they met their younger men. With their children well into adolescence, college or out of the house altogether, these older women had their first opportunities in twenty or more years to focus on themselves and their younger partners. They were able to continue their careers and enjoy the addition of love and romance to their lives.

Of the 20 percent still involved in the active child-rearing process, the path to negotiation took many forms. Each couple sought to find a balance between work, children and partnership that worked for them.

As dual income families in this modern cross-generational prototype, the older women and younger men in our sampling had to negotiate and agree upon one major point; they jointly decided to make their family life a *priority* in all the decision-making processes. Both the older woman and younger man had to agree to sacrifice a certain amount of individual career advancement for the sake of their children and the joint involvement they would share in their children's lives.

Having learned from the initial phases of the women's movement, when women were free to work, but found themselves doing a "double shift" when they returned home, these couples decided to opt for more equal distribution of domestic chores and child care. The post-feminism-aged younger husbands valued closer physical and emotional bonds with their families and were willing and able to give up the status of sole income providers in order to create more cohesive family units.

In about 60 percent of the cases, the younger man's financial contribution to the home was eclipsed by that of his older wife. We questioned the possibility of resentment—wondering if it was a potential point of conflict. We found an interesting twist in the new model. In the modern value system these couples created for themselves, the contribution of the younger man's time and energy and his emotional involvement with his family were *as* important as money. Both partners felt they were equals in what they brought to the family unit and they each recognized their value in the new dynamic.

Donna, age forty-one, and Mike, age twenty-nine, are examples of this type of shift in the traditional role models. Their five-year marriage has produced two children plus an older child from Donna's first marriage. As an established and prominent partner in a large architectural firm, Donna's financial contribution to the family significantly outweighs the income Mike's current home-based computer graphics business generates. Yet she attributes her success to Mike and his willingness to be at home and to care for the children.

They have negotiated time, money and child-rearing duties and both are happy with the roles they have created for themselves. At the beginning of each year they have a "business meeting" where they decide together who will work harder, run faster and who will bring in what portion of the income. Donna turns down certain projects that take her away from home and she has been able to take time off so that Mike can grow his business. They are clear about their positions with each other and clear as to their true goals: a strong, unified family. Donna has also been clear with her partner at work and she is in a position to take on those clients that keep her close to home and to turn down projects that would require too many long hours. Mike is an example of an evolved modern man who is willing to put his ego aside and give up the status of primary breadwinner.

Many of these "new men" have turned their backs to our culture's traditional measurements of work-life accomplishments in order to more actively participate in family life. They are shifting into a revised definition of a "man"—with a different type of contribution based on sharing, rather than having all the chips. For men who are willing to explore this new role, there are great rewards to be found in having daily interaction with their children. These "new men" enjoy being active catalysts in their children's growth and development and they value their home lives.

Mike recalled watching his father step in and out of his boyhood life as though he was a visitor. In Mike's case, those early experiences of feeling separate and apart from "the man who came home and ate dinner with us" made Mike determined to do things differently. When he met Donna, he discovered she shared the same intensity of feelings regarding the necessity for a close family unit. Having had little emotional involvement with her first husband, Donna was determined (if she married again) to find a man capable of emotional intimacy, who would also be an integral part of her daughter's life.

Another example of a couple who has negotiated a new model of balancing the demands of work and children is Vanessa, age forty-four, and Bruce, age thirty-one. Both are educators and met at work. Vanessa wasn't planning on having children of her own until she met Bruce. The emotional gratification she received from being a teacher gave her the connection she craved, but the addition of Bruce to her life made her reconsider her choices. Bruce had always wanted children. When they decided to marry, they agreed upon a system that would work for both of them.

Vanessa loved working as a teacher and this was a priority for her. Bruce also loved teaching. Together, they drafted a plan to incorporate a joint work schedule that would effectively allow them to raise a family. Vanessa would work during the first part of her pregnancy, then take time off. Bruce would be available in the summer months and during the school year Vanessa would be able to tutor privately in the late afternoon and evening hours when Bruce was at home.

The plan worked. They have two sons and both parents have been available to jointly participate in the boys' lives. Also, the domestic responsibilities have been divided. Their mornings begin with a family breakfast, at which time Bruce and Vanessa review the day's upcoming schedule and negotiate "who will do what."

Most of us today are participating in a social revolution. Like all people caught in the middle of an enormous shift, we are on unstable ground. Future generations will work out new systems of partnership and revise the existing models of relationship norms, but for those of us living through the experience now, the price of evolution is temporary disorientation. We can't look to our former relationship models to guide us through this transition.

Couples must carve their own paths and discover, through trial and error, what works for them. Each newly acquired freedom exacts a price. For women, the addition of financial power and personal status demands greater self-reliance and individual responsibility. We no longer look to men to be the "beasts of burden" and solely support the family unit. For men, the price of "wholeness" (incorporating both the masculine and feminine polarities) demands great courage. They must be willing to release the antiquated male expectations of absolute power and control and embrace new models of sharing and equality.

The cross-generational couples we have interviewed are modern day examples of the new archetype of equality that is still under construction. They are aware of the old model of power and have chosen to create a new system of egalitarianism that resonates with their evolving consciousness. They are the hallmark of a new vision of partnership.

Chapter 12

It's Only About Sex, Isn't It?

Unless it's a one-night stand, relationships are never only about sex.
Sylvia Rosenfeld, CSW

Point to an identifiably older woman/younger man couple and ask someone what he or she thinks. Chances are the person will reply that of course it's about sex (maybe the person will smile knowingly or even snicker as he or she says it.) This, like assumptions about gay or mixed race couples, is a very demeaning supposition. The implication is clear: the relationship is ONLY about sex and therefore can't be anything substantial. However, like Sylvia Rosenfeld, a New York City-based relationship and sex therapist, we also had comments: just when did sexual satisfaction become a bad thing to get from a relationship? And of course there is more to these relationships than just sex. Sylvia's further comments on this subject are insightful:

> *Remember, just because he's younger than she is doesn't mean he's more of a sexual person (unless he's seventeen or eighteen). Moreover, you can't just assume that because he's younger he's a sexy stud. The additional components of the relationship might be about nurturing or mothering; it might be about a lot of things. Unless it's a one-night stand, relationships are never only about sex. When people look at an older woman/younger man couple and dismiss it as being "only about sex," they are making a negative judgment, and good sex between a couple in a relationship is always a good thing.*

Mother Nature put women at their sexual peak later in life and men at their sexual peak much earlier. Maybe we should honor and learn some lessons from her. There is a natural attraction between older women and younger men: call it a fact of biology. However, we have been socialized to not act on it: call that conditioning. Perhaps we should give Mother Nature a little more respect and recognize that social conditioning is a man-made (literally) phenomenon.

Older men, when confronted with a woman who is involved with a significantly younger man, often respond in uncomfortably predictable ways: "Oh yeah, must be the sex." "The sex must be great" (usually expressed with a leer). These remarks are immediately followed by opinions about the younger man's intelligence (or lack thereof): "How can she even talk to him?" "He's only a child, what could they possibly have in common?" Sometimes, the older man will then proceed to question the woman's sanity: "Boy, she's gotta have a few screws loose." When confronted with this type of couple, some older men will become angry and ridicule them, although never, of course, directly to the couple. Do these older men feel threatened? Yes. Replaced? Yes. Insecure? Yes. Conflicted? Yes. Angry, demoralized, rejected and fearful? Yes. Have their emotional weaknesses created a bias that society now adheres to without examining the motives behind it? Unfortunately, yes. We can remember the gross inequalities in the American workplace before the demand for equal rights for women and minorities began the struggle to balance things out. Why did those inequalities exist in the first place? Wasn't it something about power being firmly entrenched in the white, middle-aged male population? Déjà vu? Yes.

Older women in this culture are not supposed to be sexy. Yet there are many more women in their fifties and sixties (and older) who are—while not as famous as Tina Turner, Sophia Loren, Raquel Welch or Ann Margaret—still beautiful and fit, sexy and seductive. However, we rarely see them modeling in lingerie ads or decked out in slinky little dresses selling products in magazines. We know that there is a rapidly growing market for older women in the modeling business, but we mostly see these women in advertisements for menopause-related products like hormone balancing creams, wrinkle reducing makeup or adult disposable diapers.

Rarely do we see older women selling anything that's outright sexy, revealing or body conscious. This would be too threatening to the commonly accepted view that older women and sexuality don't mix. Older women, no matter how beautiful and in shape, are not supposed to be seen as sexy. It's taboo. Disturbing. In some people's minds, disgusting. It is also a mind-set that serves the needs of insecure older men.

Older single men themselves often choose younger women. Their hostility toward older women who choose younger men seems to indicate the belief, "We don't want you, because you're not young and pretty. But even though we don't want you, we don't want anyone else to want you either." It's as if they want to be able to reject us, discard us and then control our freedom to find someone else to love us. We don't think this is fair.

New information about nutrition, the explosion of the fitness industry and newly available scientific/technological advances enable women, if we work at it, to remain strong, healthy and visibly fit well into our later years. We have seen women body builders in their eighties with figures that the average twenty-five-year-old would envy. Still, these women are denied a sexual identity, or worse, ridiculed for having one. While it is discouraging, it's not very surprising that the English language contains many more pejorative words to describe older women than it does older men.

The prevailing consciousness seems determined to keep mature women locked into some unappealing stereotypes, no matter how much the reality defies and contradicts those images. We would like to change that, as would a lot of the younger men we've spoken to. It's no wonder that the sight of an older woman with a much younger man is such a slap in the face to the population of middle-aged men who still wield power in the world, but who are also very aware of how quickly that power is being usurped. The idea that an older woman is having really great (meaning frequent and energized) sex (one of the first assumptions the sight of an older woman/younger man couple usually conjures up in the minds of others) is really the ultimate threat to older men since they're the ones who lose their sexual power as they age. A 1999 report from the *Journal of the American Medical Association* on sexual dysfunction in the United States spells it out quite clearly:

> For women, the prevalence of sexual problems tends to decrease with increasing age.... Increasing age for men is positively associated with experience of erection problems and lacking desire for sex.

Despite Viagra, when they criticize and ridicule, older men are really saying, *How dare you have great natural sex, especially when I have erectile problems.* It's a power issue, an arena in which they can't win. No wonder they want to relegate mature women to sexlessness. And their hostility toward the younger men in these unions also reactivates for some their anger at being overthrown in the workplace (watch out for those young lions!).

We don't hate men. And, despite all that we've just said about their rationale in reducing mature women to a sexless state, we especially don't hate older men. What we detest are the rigid restrictions on mature females' evolution and personal empowerment that have permeated modern culture. In truth, mature men have been as unconsciously victimized by this restrictive thinking as women have. They didn't create it, per se, but most of them did not challenge it either. And why should they? It served their needs well. We feel compelled to not only challenge such false assumptions, but to reveal them for what they are. We'd like to clean the slate to create a new and healthier attitude and new options for both men and women—a win-win situation, where those who consciously choose the old archetype may do so. If it works for them, fine. Those for whom it does not work, however, should be free to choose the less traveled, but clearly emerging path of new relationship options. Nobody needs to get bricks hurled at them because they choose to love someone. The world needs more love in it, not less.

If we hated older men, we would be hating what they reflect back to us: our own aging process. We need to let go of blame and focus on the issue—that a one-sided thinking process has limited all of our choices. We value choice and the freedom that comes from making choices. We value equality. We value greater happiness and greater joy for greater numbers of people. We value broader parameters by which we define partnership. We want to level the playing field and enjoy the same expanse of freedom our older male counterparts have considered their God-given right—to select the mate we want. We want everyone to play fair.

Even in those cases where the sexual union is clearly felonious, punishment is meted out in accordance with the prevailing male driven value system. The infamous Joey Buttafuoco has sex with an underage teenage girl, spends a few months in prison and ends up with his own talk show. He becomes a celebrity. Contrast this with Mary Jo Laetorno, a woman who is mentally ill, who has sex with a teenage boy and ends up serving years of imprisonment. Yes, we know she broke parole and did it again and that's why she deserved a harsher punishment. Still, Joey is celebrated, Mary Jo is reviled.

We are not simply indulging in some older-men bashing. We know that there are some very sexy, very evolved, very "hot" older men out there. We've met some of them and we like them a lot. It's just that there aren't nearly enough of them. We, and many other older women, have observed that they are far, far fewer in number than are their female counterparts. Women have been working to develop themselves mentally, physically and spiritually because they've had to, given the enormous economic and social changes of the last thirty-odd years. Men, in that same period, have not—because they didn't believe they needed to. However, younger men whose impressionable years have occurred during this period are in greater numbers more evolved. Therefore, consciousness-wise, as well as sexually, older women and younger men are more evenly matched today than ever before.

Intimacy
In the 1999 MTV awards, multi-platinum Detroit rapper Kid Rock brought the house down with his hit song "Bawitdaba" (*Devil Without A Cause*, WEA/Atlantic/Lava). Complete with orchestral and choral accompaniment, chanting the refrain in unison with the audience, the song acknowledges the harsh life of hookers, strippers and junkies. Juxtaposed beautifully in the middle of this rendition, were the words: "Get in the pit and try to love someone."

What a fabulous line and how astonishingly poignant in context of otherwise contrary images. And isn't that the issue? With all that's happening in the world, especially the world of sex for the sake of sex, isn't love the ultimate challenge?

We both know a New York City woman who has admittedly slept with more men than she can count. This woman insists she is an "expert" on intimacy. We tried to explain that intimacy involves more than spending a weekend together, but we couldn't convince her. She thinks *sex* is intimacy. But our couples know otherwise and so do we. Intimacy involves many areas of a couple's life together, and though sex matters and matters a lot, it is not all that matters.

One of the big pluses we've heard from the older women in our research is that the younger men with whom they have relationships are much more open and receptive to working on intimacy than their former older mates. Generationally speaking, the younger group of men have grown up with a greater awareness of self-help literature and are better versed in current psychological terminology and emotional language. Our female respondents have explained that their younger partners are less threatened by the concept of "working at the relationship," and they understand that it is a healthy, normal component of modern day romance. Conversely, one of the ongoing complaints voiced by these women about their former older male partners was their lack of relationship involvement. Our female participants felt that their former husbands/boyfriends thought the relationships would take care of themselves and that their responsibility merely consisted of providing food and shelter.

While much of the outer world's interest in cross-generational relationships focuses on the sexual aspect, the older women and younger men we interviewed were clearly interested in developing all dimensions of their relationships. Yes, the sex is important, and from what we have been told, is tremendously satisfying for them, but it was *intimacy* that was cited as the powerful catalyst to really great sex lives. Our couples explained that each partner must really work at creating and enhancing intimacy.

In order to understand the nature of intimacy, we must first be clear on what it is and what it isn't. Intimacy is not:

1. A deep, involved, intense conversation with the paperboy.
2. A sun-drenched, late afternoon drink with the pool boy.
3. A three-hour conversation with that gorgeous, rock-hard personal trainer at your health club, while you pretend you really wanted to become a professional fitness model (at age fifty).
4. One slow dance together at the disco with the dark, mysterious young man who caught your eye.
5. A wild weekend with someone who's first and last name elude you two days later.

6. A six-month relationship with the man of your dreams, but whom you only saw four times.
7. The one-time sexual encounter you *still* refer to as your "soul mate."
8. Discovering you both share the same astrological sign.
9. The half hour or so you are lying in bed, "just talking" in between intercourse.
10. Having breakfast together the morning after.

Intimacy starts with the self. It is based on accurate knowledge of who we are—who we really are—and being able to decode and decipher what we feel. Self-honesty and having a strong sense of our own identity are fundamental requirements. We also need to feel safe and secure enough within ourselves to be open and vulnerable with our mates; to reveal ourselves as both strong and weak, courageous and fearful, adult and childlike. Intimacy involves trust. We must be able to trust ourselves and trust that we can truly be ourselves with our partner and that they are safe to be themselves with us.

Dr. Marcella Bakur Weiner, New York City clinical psychologist and author, gives us an excellent overview of the nature of intimacy and helps us understand what challenges are involved in overcoming potential blocks to greater intimacy:

> *Intimacy in love relationships is as necessary to both men and women as the oxygen we breathe. But can everyone be intimate, both emotionally and sexually? Intimacy is a problem for those of us who have not attained a sense of identity. When one fears the loss of one's identity—by merging with the other person, becoming one with them, losing that precious piece of you which you feel is all you have—that person begins to move away from intimate relationships, in friendships and in love/sexual bondings.*

One of the many valuable qualities the older women we have known and interviewed have achieved is that they do have clear senses of their own identities. Their additional years of life experience have illuminated their true personalities. As we've said before, with an older woman, a younger man knows what he's getting. She has long left the stage of being confused and knows exactly what she wants. She is grounded and has had time to solidify. Overwhelmingly, the younger men in our research appreciate this quality and repeatedly make comments such as, "She knows who she is," and "She knows what she wants." This factor, we and they feel, adds stability to their relationships.

Although intimacy starts with the self, it requires the involvement of both partners. Relationship problems are exacerbated when one partner seeks greater closeness and the other partner doesn't. Relationships are in peril when both partners give up on the intimacy process. While it is a sad thing to see a loveless relationship, characterized by mutual distance and detachment, it is sadder yet to be in one.

Recently, there have been numerous books, classes and workshops available to couples who seek to improve their intimacy skills. Sylvia Rosenfeld, earlier quoted in this chapter, teaches one such course. Many private individuals, colleges and other learning institutions now offer workshops for couples who seek to enhance their love life.

No matter at which end of the intimacy spectrum your relationship lies, we urge you to explore many avenues of self and joint growth. Even if you already have a great relationship, you and your mate have the ability to make it even better.

- Explore courses and workshops that resonate for both of you.
- Check out the Internet. It is filled with all sorts of helpful information, and often includes commentary from others regarding their success and experience in this area.
- Check out your local bookstore. There are huge sections these days devoted to "Self Help" and "Relationship" issues.
- Form or find a couples' group discussing ways to improve intimacy.

Dr. Weiner offers the following advice for keeping intimacy and passion alive in your partnership:

Recognize that you are a "we," a couple, and not just the "me" you were at birth. You want to work things out on a day-to-day basis. But each of you has spent many years being your own person and now there are two of you to think of. How can you get past the petty things that crop up for all of us every day? For one, back off on criticism. Be forgiving. Forgiveness means that you open your heart to the other person. Holding on to flaws you perceive in your partner—and who doesn't have them?—means you are holding on to anger. You are a slave to it. Releasing that anger sets you free. It frees you emotionally so that you can concentrate on the positive parts of your life. When you lose your cool, two simple words can help: "I'm sorry." And breathe the free air. Your body will also release the toxins that anger puts in. What if you don't get angry too often? Great. Another way in which you can enhance your relationship is to show appreciation. Somehow, over a long period of time of living with someone or sometimes even a short time, we tend to take that person for granted. Whereas we would always say "please" and "thank you" to strangers or to the waitstaff at restaurants, we often neglect our loved ones. Take time out. Show your gratitude. This affirms your awareness of your loved one's existence and appreciation that somehow, through this miracle of discovering one other, you both ended up together.

Chapter 13

Communication in the Bedroom

I thought I was having sex with a wall.
He was totally detached...a thousand miles away...
Martha (age 50)

How does an older woman contribute to making a relationship with a younger man work in the bedroom? The answer is the same as with any other kind of relationship: commit to communication. Of course, such couples have as many problems as anyone else and some of them probably will be age related. One problem may be what sex and relationship therapist Sylvia Rosenfeld calls a tendency toward self-centeredness and the presumption that:

"If I want something, my partner must want it too." This presumption can be damaging. When you have people that are different, whether from different backgrounds, different cultures or different ages, you're coming from a totally different place. So the way an older person looks at something is different from the way a younger person looks at it. There's more room there for conflict.

The fact that the age difference does create greater opportunity for conflict means that both partners have a greater responsibility to be conscientious. They need to be aware that each may see things differently and they need to talk about such matters openly. Older people (especially those with a strong religious upbringing) might be less open, for instance, to the idea of oral sex than younger people. Years ago this was a subject that a lot of people felt very uncomfortable even talking about, much less doing. Today, the dynamics of intimacy, especially among younger couples, have become more open, more experimental, more consensual. Thus, a couple of mixed age, coming from different backgrounds and eras, must create for themselves a mutually pleasurable intimate relationship.

Sylvia Rosenfeld reminds us that we not only make false negative assumptions about the older woman/younger man couple, but some positive ones as well:

> It's easy to assume that because he's younger, he's the more playful, more adventurous one in the relationship. We presume that he needs more nurturing and, of course, that he's the more sexual partner. But the younger man may just be the more serious person, the nurturer or the more repressed one in the bedroom. How many times have we heard an older spouse say about their younger mate, "Oh, she/he's the more mature one around here"?

Our own interviews confirm that in some cases the younger man is more mature.

> He is one of those rare individuals who was born with a ninety-year-old's experience and maturity level. One of the qualities I most admired when I met him initially was the degree of wisdom he demonstrated. Although he had a great capacity for fun, I would venture to say that his level of maturity exceeded my own.
>
> **Alana (age 58)**

> Jim is much more mature...he's really the adult in our relationship. He is stable, methodical and analytical. But it's great for me, because I get to relax. I can afford to be more spontaneous and childlike. After years of being a full-time mother (to my children as well as former husband), I can finally lean on someone else.
>
> **Julia (age 49)**

It is widely believed that younger men make better lovers than older men. Certainly many younger men are more virile and sexually energetic. Rarely is their sexual performance impaired by prescription medication or their physical movements restricted due to chronic ailments. Guaranteed, your twenty-five-year-old lover will chase you around the bedroom a lot longer than your sixty-five-year-old...but does all this equate to great sex?

We know that energy and endurance aren't the only things that make a man a great lover. Great sex has a lot to do with the man's sensitivity, patience, willingness (and ability) to delay his own gratification in order to satisfy the woman. These are the attributes that an older woman can help her young lover learn, improve and master. Of course, she also needs considerable patience and sensitivity in order to instruct him without injuring his delicate ego.

Communication

If you are a woman involved with a very young man, you may be the first woman in his life who has ever explained to him what you need in bed. Maybe he's a naturally great lover and understands that sex is for the enjoyment of both partners. Maybe he's only been with girls/women his own age who haven't acquainted him with the need for romance, foreplay and delayed gratification. Very young women are usually either not yet fully aware of their sexual needs and desires or are more insecure about expressing them. It isn't surprising that the 1999 *Journal of the American Medical Association's* report on sexual dysfunction in the United States found that, "Sexual problems are most common among young women and older men."

As in any sexual relationship, you will have to communicate what you want and what turns you on. Do so in ways that are sensitive and caring. If he is unaware of how best to satisfy you, you can teach and develop your intimate relationship at the same time.

Be direct, yet gentle. Show him what you like and create room to discover what you both like. Make sure to encourage him, treat failure humorously and, above all else, be kind. Even if you had been with the same man for twenty-five years and your young lover has had numerous sexual partners, in his mind, you're probably still more experienced. Take the lead if necessary.

Many of the women we interviewed who were happily married to or living with much younger men told us about how their sexual experiences together developed and deepened over time. Clearly the emotional safety offered by stable and committed relationships enabled these couples to work through the issues that had made some of their early physical connections somewhat less than wonderful. This was a subject that provided us with plenty of shared laughter as the women described their early encounters in the bedroom. The anecdotes turned serious and heartwarming as they also recounted how their developing intimacy then enabled those early episodes to become transcendent opportunities for expressing love for their partners—and vice versa.

A good 40 percent of the young men we heard about or talked to were terrified by their first sexual encounters with older women. They assumed these women knew all sorts of things they didn't. They were afraid they wouldn't measure up. Their sexual encounters were less than stellar.

The first time was terrible. So was the second and third. I thought that maybe he had a sexual problem. It was enough that he was so young and I got myself into this in the first place, but on top of that, I figured it was over before it began and I'd made a huge mistake. I never realized he was just nervous. It felt like he was having some kind of spasm or something. I finally grabbed his butt and steered him. I said, "Glenn, like this...." I had to do it. I couldn't take it anymore.

Miriam (age 44)

When time is taken to effectively communicate, the rewards can be great.

Wow, did he come a long way. He didn't even know what foreplay was. I had to tell him! Guess those youngsters he'd been with didn't dare speak up or maybe they didn't know. He learned fast and he became a great lover. In about a year, he was a super stud. Then it became absolute bliss. By the fourth and fifth year it was like a spiritual experience—everything was there. We knew each other's bodies so well and knew what each other liked. We were really connected on every level and it came out full blast in the bedroom.

Elaine (age 47)

At first, I thought I was having sex with a wall. He was totally detached and just hammered me. I felt he was a thousand miles away. It took a lot of work and a lot of really honest communication. I didn't know how to hook his feelings into the physical act. When he finally got it, everything changed. It was like I had a whole new partner. He was loving, verbal and expressive. He totally got into it and was completely present. What an incredible experience. I don't think a lot of guys know how to totally be there. As our relationship grew, he learned to be an exceptionally caring lover.

Martha (age 50)

You will need to draw upon your knowledge of yourself to be confident and verbal enough to explain these things in a sensitive way to your partner. If you have a gift for nonverbal communication, you can use it to your best advantage—and his.

Satisfying physical intimacy not only requires knowledge of self, knowledge of partner and good communication skills, but a desire to share in the experience of mutual joy. Rewarding sexual intimacy is based upon both partners feeling fulfilled. There is a dance of give-and-take, of offering and receiving. The act of physical lovemaking, when satisfying to both partners, is a form of communication within itself. It is another language with which we express our closeness and appreciation for our partners. It is based upon a sense of deep connection and bonding. The day-to-day events we share with our partner help to reinforce that bond. The physical act of expressing that bond requires trust as well as vulnerability. Both partners need to feel safe enough to communicate their desires without judgment or shame.

This has been, traditionally, a much more difficult passage for women than men. Many of us grew up with the impression that "ladies" politely submit to the sexual desires of their mates and that their job was to provide satisfaction for their men. The sexual revolution of the 1960s and 1970s allowed women to share in the experience of mutual pleasure. And while many women may not have shared fulfilling sexual experiences, maturity and reflection have allowed many of these women to gain greater knowledge of their own needs and desires.

One of the great benefits of aging (or growing up) is, for those who gain insight, the release of restrictions we have placed upon ourselves. We gain freedom as we mature. We are no longer held in place by societal ideology. As women evolve and mature, they release the restrictive "shoulds" and become much more comfortable with who they are. While most young women in their twenties are still learning what they like, women well into their thirties and beyond clearly know what works for them and have come to points in their lives where they are not afraid to express themselves.

When young men told us what turns them on about older women when it comes to sex, the same theme was repeated over and over and over again. It was the confidence and security factor:

> *She knew what she wanted.*
> *She wasn't afraid to say what she wanted.*
> *She didn't play games. Just came right out and told you what she wanted.*
> *She knew what she liked and didn't like—and she didn't hesitate to tell me.*
> *She knew who she was, no coy nonsense, no games.*
> *Young women are just too insecure, always making you work to figure out what they really want, probably because they don't even know.*

They went on and on. We concluded that an older woman who is secure in herself, knows what she wants and has the confidence to express it is sexually attractive to a younger man. Many of the young men with whom we spoke also expressed their appreciation for having equal partnerships in bed as well as out. The onus of pleasurable sex was not entirely theirs.

Dr. Patrick Suraci, a clinical psychologist in private practice in Manhattan, confirms that:

> *A younger man may feel more comfortable allowing an older woman to take charge of the sexual activity. With a younger woman, he may feel more of an obligation to initiate the sexual activity and more responsible for her pleasure. He expects an older woman to know what she likes and to be more direct in asking for it. Women generally become more comfortable with their own sexuality as they age. Therefore, the older woman and younger man may be more compatible in negotiating sexual activity.*

Love, as in any relationship, is the most important factor. If an older woman and younger man truly love each other, there is a good chance that the relationship will work. The older woman can facilitate the development of stability, which a younger man may be seeking. If love drives the sexual activity, the couple can attain mutual satisfaction.

We had heard similar ideas from the women to whom we spoke, of course, but were delighted to have a male therapist back us—and our interviewees—up.

I was just "getting off" before Linda. It didn't matter who the girl was— it was all the same. They were just bodies. Then with Linda, there was a whole person inside.

Peter (age 25)

I'm not one of those Psychic Hotline people—the woman has to tell me or do something to let me know what works for her. I guess I'm "converted" now. I only want an adult woman. They know who they are—in and out of bed. I did the other route...looks great, but it's all show.

Greg (age 36)

Her Issues
On the other hand, if the woman doesn't feel good about herself, especially about the signs of age she sees in her body, this can be a serious problem.

Nothing is more of a turnoff than when a woman feels uptight about her looks in bed. I've been with beautiful women who act this way—young women. It kills the whole thing. Some older women understand this and they are considered great lovers...not because they are older, but they've learned this fact.

Phillipe (age 37)

Phillipe's theory that the woman who is self-confident, not because of physical beauty and youth but the aura inside, was repeated in many of our interviews with young men involved with mature women. Physical love is enhanced when both people want to please each other, not just themselves.

What I like with Margaret is how she involves herself in all aspects in bed. She's not shy or withdrawn. She's totally there—with me. That's a real aphrodisiac for a man. Women don't understand this—they think it's all about the body. If they really knew this, they'd all enjoy themselves a lot more.

Craig (age 43)

Women do, as we well know, have more body image issues than men. Even a recent television commercial spoofed us by showing a group of macho-type guys in a bar looking into the camera and bemoaning the size of their thighs and asking if they looked fat in the pants they were wearing. It's a very funny commercial, but the reality isn't so funny. Poor body image is why many more females suffer from eating disorders than males. It accounts for the enormous size of the diet industry (which caters mostly to women) and why we are more obsessed with fighting cellulite than we are with serious issues. The emphasis on youth, beauty and thinness in our culture denigrates women and the problem gets worse as we get older.

Psychotherapist Kathleen Calabrese confirms:

> *Our culture bombards us with images of sickly, wan, ghostlike young women and holds them up as the ideal female form. Hence, it takes time for women to realize their true value.*

Under the best of circumstances—like when we're covered by fashionable clothing—many women are still unsatisfied with their bodies and looks. Now add the age factor and nudity to this equation and you can see the potential for high anxiety. Most mature women can relate to this. How often have we sat or laid in bed, practicing posing in front of a mirror so that we'd look better? We suck in our stomachs. We fold our arms close in to our bodies to make our breasts look bigger, rounder, fuller. We've learned from popular comedy routines that it's better to exit a room walking backward. Men in battle are advised, "Don't let them see the whites of your eyes." Women are told, "Don't let them see your behind."

When it comes to sex, especially, we become all the more self-conscious. Even women who have taken excellent care of themselves and stayed in good physical shape are familiar with the fear experienced by a woman the first time she's about to be intimate with a man. *How will I look? Will he like my body? Will he find me attractive physically?* All women share these concerns to some extent, but when a woman is older and she has a new lover who is considerably younger, the normal concerns are exacerbated.

Thoughts like, *Will he be excited by me or will my body turn him off?* pervade our thinking. Instead of reaching an age at which we can finally enjoy and be comfortable with our sexual maturity, we bombard ourselves with the pressures of our highly body-conscious society. Do our older male counterparts obsess about their flaws in the same way? Usually when an older, paunchy, out-of-shape but successful man takes off his shirt, he's probably not thinking, *Oh God. My abs aren't ripped. Maybe she'll see my love handles. I better lower the lights so she won't see the cellulite on my stomach.* Women tend to apologize for their perceived flaws: "I'm usually ten pounds thinner than this, it's just that I've been under stress. I can take it off easily." Do men ever apologize for their bodies? Rarely.

Don't apologize. Accept yourself. If you are about to enter into a sexual relationship with a younger man, remember you have the wisdom and maturity to have weeded out those who simply want sex and recognized who wishes to have a deeper relationship. By the time you're ready to hit the sheets, there will already be an emotional (we hope a loving) connection between you.

Don't compare, enjoy. If he is in better physical shape than you are, so what? We have also known the reverse to be true, where the older woman is in much better shape than her younger man. A number of the women with whom we talked had chosen young men who were either quite overweight, painfully thin or just lacking any musculature. In these cases it was the older woman in the relationship who was the inspiration for the man to improve his physical appearance.

As you surely know, men have for years been practicing the fine art of envisioning us naked while we are fully clothed. Do you really believe your young man will be surprised when he sees you naked for the first time? Do you think he hasn't already imagined you in that state? The desire and ability to do this appears to come encoded in the male gene. No matter how much those control-top pantyhose hold you in, he probably has a pretty good idea how you look—and he likes it.

The young man is there because he wants to be with you. Stop focusing on the comparison of bodies and age. Allow yourself to be involved in your relationship. Men don't really notice what we think they notice. We knew a woman, Darlene, who actually felt the need to explain to her young man that she had varicose veins on the backs of her legs. He had no clue as to what she was talking about. She described to us how she kept pointing to the backs of her legs and showing him so he could see what she was talking about. He still didn't notice. Darlene told us how frustrated she became by his apparent inability to see her flaw. She had said, "See! See! See! Look! They're all over! See these blue things! They're varicose veins. I have them all over. Look! See, here's another one. I *told* you I had varicose veins."

After fifteen minutes of her pointing, highlighting and explaining, she finally convinced the young man that she did, indeed, have varicose veins. Unbelievable! Meanwhile, he didn't care, didn't see them and would never have known about them if it weren't for her determined insistence. Don't point out your perceived flaws. Don't apologize or explain about how out of shape you are. He doesn't see it. When men are sexually excited, they see what they want to see, and they fantasize that it looks the way they want it to look.

Young men who want relationships with older women are not looking for varicose veins, ingrown hairs or how much fat you think you have on your stomach. They have been attracted by the whole package. All systems are go. He doesn't have the time or interest to scrutinize your body, hunting for flaws. Let yourself flow with the sexual energy. Stay in the moment, enjoy him and what you share. Allow this to be an opening for physical, spiritual and emotional union and put your thoughts on hold.

We've been exposed many times to the idea that we do a lot better in our lives when we love ourselves. It's one of those life lessons once again confirmed by our research. So you've got some wrinkles, some flab, some gray in your hair. So what? Stop worrying and unleash your sex-goddess self. Stop fretting that he'll dump you as soon as he meets some young thing. He already knows plenty of young things and he doesn't want them. He wants you. You turn him on.

Your obsessing about being older isn't fun for him either. Alex, one of our male interviewees, told us that his biggest turnoff is an older woman who constantly compares herself to young women and asks him why he would be with her when he could easily attract someone much younger.

> *A forty-seven-year-old woman should not try to compete with a twenty-seven-year-old. There's no competition. If an older woman is ashamed of her body and doesn't feel good about showing it, the sex can't be good. If she is insecure about her body, it's a turnoff. If she tries to look and act like a young girl, it shows she's insecure. It shows she doesn't like herself. It's not a good feeling for the man she's with.*
>
> **Alex (age 39)**

His Issues
Just as often, though, it's the young man who's the insecure one, especially if it's their first time together. Perhaps he's thinking that she's been there, done that and knows the difference between mediocre, good and great. He thinks he's got to show her what a stud muffin he is.

> *We first made love in the dead of winter. It was really cold out. He kept trembling and I just thought he was cold. Later, he told me he was terrified. He thought of me as this incredibly sexual older woman who'd experienced lots of men. He'd had more sexual partners than I had, but he was afraid of how he'd measure up. It's so funny now when I think of his reaction—assuming I'd had tons of sexual experience just because I'm older.*
>
> **Gail (age 41)**

> *Our first time together was a wipeout. Thank God it turned out to be just nerves on his part.*
>
> **Jean (age 52)**

Talk about performance anxiety! At least one-third of the couples we spoke to described their first encounter as awkward and basically unsuccessful. So what should a woman do if the effort fails? Laugh it off. No big deal. Try again later.

Don't worry if the first few times sexual encounters are nerve-ridden and tense. If the fire is there, the energy is electric and every time you speak to each other you are energized and relaxed, that's all you need. Love yourself. Express yourself. Enjoy the ride.

The road to physical love requires a healthy degree of self-knowledge and successful intimacy requires communication, trust and time. Given that the older women in our research have had more years in which to learn about themselves and have chosen to discard many socially imposed restrictions, the mutual attraction and passion they are able to share with their younger mates is often truly intense and mutually satisfying. In such relationships older women have a great advantage that is working in their favor. They are finally free to delight in the totality of being themselves.

In speaking to Linda, age fifty-one, and her husband, Carl, age thirty-eight, we clearly felt the intense passion they enjoyed. Although these two had been married twelve years, they acted like newlyweds. They glowed. There was an electricity in the air, especially when they spoke about their love life. Carl explained:

> Linda is my soul mate...I know it now and I knew it then (when we met). The minute I saw her, I knew there was something different. When I heard her voice...I knew that voice. It was a wild feeling...I wasn't expecting to find her so soon. I was in my late twenties and I had a whole map of how it would happen. But there she was and I just knew it. People always say, "You'll just know." And I heard that a lot and thought it was fantasy, but when I met her, I did know.

Carl works in the construction industry and was, as he told us, very traditional and old-fashioned. He wanted to make sure he had enough money to feel comfortable with a wife and family before he found the woman of his dreams. He had laid out an entire scenario, a timetable, for this to happen. However, as Linda told us, she entered the picture much sooner than he anticipated:

> It wasn't all chemistry for me. Usually I knew when I met a man what it would be like, but with Carl, I can only say, looking back, that I was very, very interested. I wanted to be around him, to be near him. That was a new feeling for me.

As Linda and Carl spoke about their love life, they communicated to us the deep, loving connection they shared. They had spent a lot of time and energy working on their relationship, developing themselves and communicating with each other. They are what we would term an evolved couple. They have attended workshops and seminars to enhance their relationship, made time to have "special dates" and vacations in romantic settings and they actively acknowledge that they strive to not only keep the passion alive, but to cultivate it. They are typical of a new breed—the kind of conscious individuals who understand that meaningful relationships require work and attention. They both agree that it doesn't "just happen." Carl told us what he feels he needs to do:

> *When I was young, sexual excitement was a temporary thing. I would feel it, experience it, then it was gone. I have learned that I can maintain that feeling—but it takes some effort. Not work per se, but effort, or at least, focus. I have to tune into Linda, listen to her, and we both make sure we communicate with each other. That's really important.*

When we began to discuss the nature of passion, both Carl and Linda visibly lit up in front of our eyes. They told us that their passion gets more intense with the years and they both found it strange that so many couples claim that passion fades with time. Linda was especially vocal on this topic:

> *If you're doing the right things, there should be more passion and greater excitement. Think about it: You really know the person you are with...you have gone through so many things, so many ups and downs, and you feel closer because of it. I think what really trips people up is when there is a hurt or a resentment that isn't addressed. If it is there, it is like an open wound. It doesn't go away. In fact, it gets worse unless you take care of it. Then, there are more wounds—it creates a wall over time. Those couples, they don't talk, you see, they don't get the problems out, and so they begin to feel a coldness set in. That comes out in their sex life. Especially for women, when we are hurt, we shut down sexually. I think that's what happens to those people. They just shut down and stop trying to reach out to each other.*

Dr. Marcella Bakur Weiner, clinical psychologist, takes this idea even further. About keeping the passion alive, she advises:

> *Do some special little things not just for holidays and birthdays, but during the week, on a no-special-anything-but-just-because "I love you" basis. In our super-hyped society, we may sometimes forget that people always*

were and will be just people and all of us need appreciation. It reminds us of the "mirroring" we had from good parenting, the way in which a mother/father/caretaker looked at us, took notice of who we were, what we were saying, doing, wearing. It made us feel special. They took time out just for us. Do a little something. It need not cost much money—a little creativity will do. Plan a picnic—on your living room floor. Buy some flowers, play some glorious music, burn some incense if you are so inclined. Open up a bottle of fresh wine and under the blanket spread out on your floor, place a small gift, wrapped in exotic paper, no matter what its size or cost, and give it—with a kiss. Tell your partner how much you care. It need not take a long time, but it goes a long way. The rewards are stupendous.

When we asked Linda and Carl what advice they could offer to our readers to keep the passion alive, Linda jumped right in:

Communicate. Don't let anger or hurt or resentment build up. Try something else we both do...we act like we are still dating. We really try to please each other, to excite each other. We explore new things, we take a chance on doing things that just come to us and it really works. I think the worst thing people do is that they settle down with each other and stop trying. They look at marriage like the end—now I've got him or her—and they quit trying to be lovers. A lot of couples have the attitude that they've finally "caught" someone so now their work is done. On the contrary, that's when it should begin.

Dr. Weiner concurs:

The biggest turnoff in couples is when one thinks the other has to do/act/feel and say as they do. Respect the differences. Mix them, as you would two colors, into each other at times and admire them as separate hues at other times. That will keep your passion and your partner's constantly charged. Remember, passion is life. Live it!

One thing all of our couples have found: they truly enjoy and relish the physical aspect of their love. Of the more than two hundred people we interviewed and researched, a total 100 percent of our respondents claimed the sex life in their mixed age relationship was the greatest they had experienced to date. Our older women and younger men have hit upon something that obviously works for them. They all were immensely satisfied with their love life and expressed the incredible joy of finding both a wonderful partner and gratifying lover. It seems to come with the territory. The chemistry between older women and younger men is not only intense, but often also contains the capacity for a long-term committed relationship. Along with their mutual love and respect for each other, the committed couples to whom we've talked seem to be some of the best examples of relationships that can, and do, work.

Mother Nature

Throughout the centuries, humanity has looked to nature to reveal the laws of the universe. This innate, divine system of natural order creates life and brings death. The seasons change and species evolve. Nature's wisdom has guided us throughout time in an ever-changing world.

Yet, while it is apparent to social scientists and sexual researchers that a man's sexual peak rises between his teens and twenties and a woman's at mid-life, many people seem confused and amazed that these two groups seek to unite. But why, we ask, did Mother Nature create this potent similarity in sexual appetites?

We believe there is often a natural attraction between younger men and older women. The sexual passion of the younger man and older woman are perfectly matched. There can be phenomenal sex between them, according to the couples we've researched. Even as they age together, their sexual energies seem to stay in alignment. And there is a lot more than just sex in alignment. The relationship between the younger man and older woman matures as does their passion for each other. Though they age at different times, in different ways the love between them grows and prospers.

The older woman has a better sense of herself. She is more fully developed. She is the rose in full bloom, with all the fragrance and majesty of her life force revealed. And young men desire her. Their desire for the totality of who she is expresses itself as sexual attraction.

Chapter 14

Giving Yourself Permission

I remember thinking the whole time, I really like this guy,
but he's young and he's a struggling musician. I can't be doing this.
Liz (age 54)

Since you are reading this book, chances are that you have thought about or imagined entering into a relationship with a younger man, are currently involved with a younger man or were involved with a younger man and wished you'd had some kind of guidance. We, too, have learned through trial and error. We've relied on the wise counsel of our female friends, as well as our own intuition and wisdom. We have written this book in order to share what we've learned.

One of the things we learned is that there are few if any Mrs. Robinsons. The concept of this fictional character, popularized in the wonderful movie *The Graduate*, is not representative of the women we know, the participants of our research or ourselves. The image of the sex-starved middle-aged woman luring an innocent young man into her bed is pure fantasy...pressed onto celluloid. It's just not based in reality.

Among our friends and acquaintances, and among the many women we interviewed for this book, we know of no one who intentionally set out to capture a much younger man. Neither we nor they resorted to control, manipulation or any devious tactics to entice young men into their arms. Nobody crashed Eagle Scout Jamborees, cruised the local high school parking lots or hung out in college bars. We didn't instigate, plot or plan strategies to hunt young men down. In most cases, just the opposite was true.

Steve, who was twenty-two, was totally nuts when we first met. He was acting off the wall, coming on to me and telling me he was going to come over to my house the next day so I could cook him chicken parmigiana! I didn't know him and told him to get lost, but he wouldn't let up. He was so persistent, it was funny. I thought he was showing off for his friends and I ignored him. Then I saw him again about a week later and he was more serious. But again with the chicken parmigiana! He was cute, but I didn't see the point. He was just way too young. Then I ran into him again— it was a joke now, with the chicken. We talked some and he was pretty interesting. He asked me for my number, and you know, I just gave it to him. It was weird because I don't do that much, but I did it this time.

He called me right away and I got a really sick feeling in my stomach, like "What have I started? I don't want this." So I said I was busy. He kept on calling. One night, he started talking about politics and the economy—and I was really surprised by how smart he was. I was supposed to go out that night with a friend who had just canceled, so I said yes to him. It was last minute. I'm glad I did it now. But I was always wondering in the beginning what he was up to, because, for me, I couldn't get why he wanted someone so much older. I thought that maybe he just wanted to try it out, to satisfy his curiosity. But he was more serious than I was. He's really the one who made it work, you know, because I just never believed it. I had thought, This has to be some kind of game. So I really didn't want to like him so much, but I did. Then I worried he was playing me—I really made myself crazy for a long time, because it was just too weird for me. But we got along fine. He was always okay with it. He said it was love at first sight for him. Not me— I took it real slow—but he's a good guy. A real good, good guy.

Stacey (age 46)

For most of us, these relationships just happened. We simply went about our day-to-day business. We went to work, the park, the health club, movies, the market and out with friends. We took our clothes to the cleaners, drove our cars and went on trips. We did what we needed to do for ourselves and did things we loved in our free time. And often, unexpectedly, he was there, too.

I was waiting in line at the supermarket. I guess I was daydreaming or something, not paying attention to what was going on around me. Suddenly, I looked up and there was this really cute young guy staring at me that way. I thought I was imagining it, but I looked at him and he gave me a big smile and continued to stare. I got nervous and looked away, but I could tell he was still looking at me. I tried to ignore him. Then he followed me out to my car and tried to make small talk. I was totally shocked when he asked for my number! I was going, "Should I, shouldn't I?"

Angie (age 47)

I first saw Michael at a group therapy meeting. He was young, but so wise. I would listen to him share each week and thought, Wow, he's someone I'd really like to know. *One day he mentioned that he was having trouble with his resume. After the meeting, I offered to look it over. That was the beginning of the best relationship I've ever had.*

Lynn (age 42)

I was always very conservative and mature for my age. At nine, I felt and acted thirty-five. Then when I was thirty-six, I ended a ten-year relationship with an older man. I felt free for the first time in my life. I began attracting young guys everywhere I went. They seemed to be coming out of the woodwork. I took the leap and began seeing a fellow who was right out of college. I felt uncomfortable and confused by my behavior and I asked my therapist what was going on. She explained that I was completing a developmental stage in my life and not to worry. It would pass and not take the equal amount of years. Well, she was wrong. I spent the next ten years in two long-term, committed relationships with younger men (sixteen and twenty years younger). Looking back, it was the best thing I ever did for myself.

Sheila (age 44)

Ray and I had been together for about ten years when I met Lloyd. The relationship with Ray was pretty much dead in the water. We had sex about once every six weeks, kind of to convince ourselves that we were still a couple. I had just turned forty and there I was: not married, in a dying relationship and very aware of the changes in my body...that middle-age spread thing.

Lloyd and I met walking our dogs in the park. We exchanged doggie owner small talk. He was very good looking. I guessed his age to be around twenty-eight. It wasn't until later that I found out he was twenty. Anyway, he was really cute and I could see that he was kind of "checking me out" when he looked at me. I wasn't really surprised by that, even though I was forty and starting to look it. I had always been considered a pretty woman. I was used to guys looking me up and down, but what got my attention was that this guy was a lot younger than what I normally attracted. Perhaps really young guys had been looking at me that way, but I just never noticed them before.

But Lloyd I noticed and we'd kind of flirt whenever we'd run into each other in the park. He finally suggested that we get together and I looked him straight in the eyes and said, "Sure, why not?" We had an affair that lasted about two years and it was great. We're still friends. That was twelve years ago, and I must say, it probably did as much for my self-esteem as a face-lift would have.

Pat (age 52)

    I'm a widow and live in an adult community. When my husband passed away four years ago, I became very depressed. We had a wonderful marriage, family life and active social involvements. After a few months, the cards and phone calls stopped. Our friends disappeared. I was very sad and alone.

    The few gentlemen I did meet were well into their seventies, quite frail and in poor health. I didn't want to nurse a sick man. I decided that if I had to be alone, I'd try to make the best of it. I started taking classes at the community center. They offered a line-dancing course. I was a good dancer in my day, so I tried it.

    Allan was the instructor. He was helpful and paid a lot of attention to me. At first I thought he was just being nice to this old gal. When he asked me to go out with him at the end of the course, I blushed like a schoolgirl. He was much younger.

Ann (age 70, involved with Allan, age 59)

Of the women with whom we talked, 80 percent had no idea that the young men in question were interested in them. They thought the men were being nice, polite or even felt sorry for them. Little did these women know the men had chosen them, desired them and wanted to be with them.

    I had just ended a seven-year relationship with an older man whom I loved, but wasn't in love with. I went to my college roommate's wedding out of town. She was the only person I knew there, and she, of course, had her hands full at the reception. I was sitting alone at a table when John came over and asked me to dance. I remember thinking how thoughtful he was and chalked it up to good manners. I figured he was taking turns dancing with all of the older single women, the grandmas, elderly aunts and me.

    He was a great dancer. I thanked him and started to return to my seat. He grabbed my hand and pulled me back to the dance floor. "One more," he said. This time I noticed his eye contact, the way he was looking at me. He had to be about twenty-two or twenty-three. His eyes went right through me and I felt this intense heat shoot straight through my body as he danced with me. I was actually feeling uncomfortable and really flustered, so I tried to go back to my seat again. I was thinking, Oh God, what should I do when a slow dance starts? He took my hand and pulled me right out of the chair. I couldn't think straight and started talking just to break the tension. I said I didn't know how to slow dance. He looked me right in the eyes and said very slowly and deliberately, "Don't worry. I know how to dance. I'll show you."

As he pulled me closer, I felt every hair follicle on my body stand on end. I was thirty-five years old and had never felt anything like this before. A door had opened before me and I walked through it that night. My life hasn't been the same since. I remember talking to my therapist about it. She said the most beautiful and unexpected thing: "It was the kiss that awakened the princess."

Victoria (age 41)

Victoria enthralled us as she described the rest of the evening's events. She and John took a romantic walk in the moonlight. Her new $250 satin pumps were ruined by grass stains and she couldn't have cared less. She stood with the young man near a pond, watching the full moon glisten in the water. Victoria reminisced:

We held hands, talked and looked at the full moon. The night was perfect...like something out of a movie. In my wildest dreams, I never thought I'd be living out this moment...but here it was and I couldn't pass it up.

Some of us are fortunate enough to discover and enter that zone of emotional freedom and openness when we are very young. Others, like Victoria, get there later in life. The methods we employ in making the choice to release the fear and repression of our socialization (especially if it has been very traditional or restrictive) parallels the mental gymnastics and gyrations necessary to give ourselves permission to leap into a socially unsanctioned relationship. Thoughts of *Should I? I can't do this, it's not right. What will people think? This is selfish. This is not respectable, it's not appropriate* roil our brains and destroy our sleep. For those who choose to leap into the unknown, however, a steel door is often blown wide open in their lives, after which they are never the same. They say yes in the face of the "No, you shouldn't" and bravely make the leap in the name of love.

Although Karolina (now eighty) and Paolo (sixty-four) have been together for twenty-five years, Karolina did not leap into a relationship with Paolo at first. In fact, as she told us, she mistook his interest as kindness toward an "old lady":

When my second husband died, he had been sick a very long time. We were living on an island. I don't drive and I needed help getting around. Paolo offered to drive me. I thought he was so nice—"How nice of him to help this old lady." I was fifty-five and he was thirty-nine then. He helped me a lot...and with many other things. He was very sweet. He would come to check up on what I needed each day. He helped in the garden, with food, things that needed fixing in the house. Maybe he wants a job, I was thinking.

In the vast majority of cases we've explored, it was the men who were in pursuit. They engaged the women in conversation, made their presence known, found excuses to see them and found reasons to help them. Most of the women missed it entirely, because their minds just didn't go there.

I met my younger man, Kevin, at our health club. He just came over one day and started talking to me. Sometimes I'd be on the bike or the Stairmaster, so we'd talk for a pretty long time. Just small talk at first, but later it got pretty philosophical—about life, relationships, things like that. He was never flirtatious or anything, just friendly. He was half my age and I was even giving him advice on picking a nice girl!

I can usually tell if a man is interested in me, but he was neutral and always respectful. I really had no clue. He was nice looking and I liked him as a person. It just never occurred to me that he was attracted to me. It wasn't until one day when he followed me out to the car—we stood in the parking lot for over an hour. Then it hit me that other male friends don't make a point to spend this much time with me.

I was reluctant, to say the least. I didn't know how to handle it. I didn't know if I should. Part of me wanted to run away, but we'd become too close for me to do that. So we talked about it. It took me a couple of weeks of wrestling with my fears, but I decided not to get involved. There were too many potential problems. I didn't want the age difference thing and I didn't want to mess up our friendship.

A couple of weeks later it was Christmas Eve and I went to a party at a friend's house (also from our health club). Kevin walked in the door. We looked at each other and I knew I'd kick myself later if I didn't give in. That was the beginning of our lengthy romance.

Barbara (age 44)

When the women finally did get it, those who decided to give themselves permission to experience a new type of relationship may have chosen to help the younger men by taking the lead. But if they did so, it was only out of the discomfort of watching the men struggle with something for which they, too, had no previous experience.

Most of the women we spoke to told us that they had initially been shocked, startled and/or confused by the younger men's attention. Many were flattered, although none were so nonchalant as to have avoided experiencing some degree of inner turmoil. *Should I? Shouldn't I?* Subtle, unspoken messages have filtered through the female consciousness that simply say, "You cannot go there." Our mothers never sat us down with the obligatory birds-and-bees talk and threw in, "Oh by the way, don't fall in love with anyone younger than yourself." No one said it, but we absorbed it subliminally, and the message was clear and definite. It's not a message that men have had to wrestle with. Indeed, historically, culturally and perhaps even biologically, men have been encouraged to choose younger mates.

For a woman, the recognition that she is attracted to the much younger man who is attracted to her involves philosophical, sociological, ethical—and sometimes religious—conflicts. Given how difficult it is these days to find someone with whom we really click, it is ironic that women do not rejoice. Instead, women greet their potential new relationships with mental turmoil, conflicted feelings and the need to weigh the psychic and emotional price of these choices. "Can we walk this walk?" we ask. "Can we take the heat?—the comments from others?—our own fears and projections?"

Sanctions against older women/younger men couples, spoken or implied, are a line drawn in the sand by the dominant culture. Some women dare not cross that line.

> *I remember thinking the whole time, I really like this guy, but he's young and he's a struggling musician. I can't be doing this. I think I was just really afraid of the response I'd get at work. I'd have to cover up and lie a lot. He didn't fit with my career. This was not an appropriate relationship for someone like myself. So I didn't allow myself to pursue it.*
>
> **Liz (age 54)**

One of our friends talked to us about an earlier time in her life:

> *I can laugh about it now, it seems so ridiculous given where my life is now. But I seriously didn't want to go out with Paul, because he was all of eight years younger than me. Never mind that he and I had everything in common, that I felt more comfortable with him than with anyone I had ever known and that he treated me better than the men I had been used to. I was embarrassed and ashamed. What would people think? I was living in a small community at that time and I had just landed a very public, very "socially important" job. I was terrified that if anyone found out, I would be diminished in their view. I was afraid that they would change their minds about me and I would lose my job. Can you imagine? But it's true, that's what I was feeling back then, the first time I thought about being with a younger guy.*
>
> **Beverly (age 61)**

It comes down to two kinds of women: Those who dare not cross the line society has invented and those who dare to leap across it. Both choices are correct for those who make them. Some lives demand comfort, normality and smooth, paved highways. Others must design their own routes in life—

tasting and experiencing the excitement of being an individual even if it means navigating over and around some bumps and potholes in the road.

For the woman who has given herself permission to ignore the sanctions and stereotypes, the price may be high, the outcome (as with any relationship) uncertain, but the goal is most worthy, being the opportunity to experience intimacy and true connection with a partner of her choosing. It is the opportunity to say yes to joy, to find a lost dream, to allow yourself to be pleasantly surprised.

> *I thought I'd never find commitment again. I was terrified at first—over forty, looking over forty—and with four children. Who would want me? And if someone did want me, would I want them? I never in my wildest dreams thought I'd be able to have more, rather than less. My relationship with Ed, or someone like Ed, was something I never envisioned. But it happened; we fell in love and we're going to be married.*
> **Connie (age 47, speaking about Ed, age 36).**

> *I always liked older men. They seemed so exciting—wiser and more knowledgeable than me. Their power and confidence was a real turn on. Then one day (I was around thirty-five), my thinking shifted. I saw these men as old, boring and used up. I saw rigid behavior, a set lifestyle and no sense of spontaneity and fun. When Mark came along, I realized I needed that spark, that life-force he possessed. All the excitement and joy came back—and every day with him was like a new day.*
> **Kathleen (age 39, speaking about Mark, age 27)**

Do these rewards outweigh the risks? Is reclaiming an exuberance lost or perhaps never experienced in your own youth worth the potential discomfort? We believe it is. But only you can decide for yourself.

Chapter 15

Taking the Lead

*If she hadn't said something first,
I'd still be looking at her and waiting for a sign.*
Alan (age 30, talking about Leslie, age 43)

We read *The Rules* by Ellen Fein & Sherrie Schneider and we applauded fervently. If only we'd had such an example of behaving from self-esteem when we were in our twenties and thirties, we probably would have done a lot of things differently, made fewer mistakes and had different, indeed, better relationships in our lives.

However, we are no longer young women and we are free to make different kinds of choices. Our goals have changed. We are seasoned. We know what we've had and—good or bad as it was for us—we don't necessarily want more of it. We are not comfortable being coy and hoping that if we can hold ourselves in check we'll be rewarded by a phone call asking us out on a date. We know what we want and we feel uncomfortable pretending otherwise. We are in charge of our lives and we don't want to give up our power. Yet when it comes to the male/female dynamic, we are still into the old, *"Oh, I hope he calls me"* mind-set. Our daughters have rejected such restrictions and so must we, particularly when it comes to dealing with younger men. If you want him to ask you out, you must help him. You must give him permission to do it!

When a younger man finds himself attracted to an older woman, he frequently sees that woman as unattainable. He sees someone who is more worldly, more experienced and more knowledgeable than himself.

106

Alan, age thirty, shared with us his hesitancy in approaching Leslie, age forty-three:

She was so beautiful, so together looking. I was scared. She was gorgeous and very friendly, but I couldn't believe she was interested in me. I thought she was just being nice. But the way she looked at me made me think she might be interested. If she hadn't said something first, I'd still be looking at her and waiting for a sign.

Ironically, at the same time the young man is feeling fearfully hesitant, the woman may be looking at herself and, seeing wrinkles, sagging breasts and cellulite, doubting any man could love her. At fifty-nine, Helena went through a crisis of self-doubt before meeting her younger man:

When I found myself single and in my fifties, I honestly believed that it was all over. The poor body image that I've lived with since being an overweight teenager only got worse. Now all the years of losing and gaining, gaining and losing weight really showed. Looking in the mirror at my body made me want to die. Who, other than a troll, would ever be attracted to me again, I wondered. "God," I prayed, "send me someone who loves my body more than I do." Then I met Xavier, who was adorable, well-built and couldn't take his hands off me. He was South American and preferred women with meat on their bones. He also preferred mature women, both mentally and emotionally. We've been together for eight years. He's thirteen years younger than I am.

The man who is interested in an older woman overlooks or is blind to her physical imperfections. He's looking at a sexy, desirable creature who can pick and choose among men who are wiser, more sophisticated, more affluent and more powerful in the world than he is. He feels anxious. *What would she want with me?* he wonders. He doesn't know that she, too, is asking herself, *What would he want with me?* But she has more power in this situation, because he has, in his mind, given it to her. He sees her as seductive, independent, able to choose whatever or whomever she wants. He is terrified to make the first move. His ego is on the line far more than it would be if he were contemplating a move toward a peer—and we all know how fragile a man's ego can be.

I never had a problem asking a girl out, but Janet wasn't a girl, she was a woman. She had everything. Culture, class, intelligence. I was frozen. This time, I knew, everything mattered. I felt like a kid. I was incredibly self-conscious, aware of my clothes, my body language, my behavior. I felt totally exposed and like everything was on the line. I just really didn't want to screw it up with her.

Peter (age 31)

Many young men may experience anxiety and a sort of nervous paralysis and they require assistance to get past it. The woman has the power and it's useless to pretend otherwise. She has to use that power if there's going to be any forward movement in the relationship. The older woman must act to take the lead, albeit with subtlety and grace. Too forceful behavior may intimidate him even more.

> *When I first met Michael, I sensed he was interested because he kept hanging around and always looking to make small talk. I knew he didn't know how to take it to the next level and I was getting tired of waiting. So, one day, I looked him straight in the eyes and said, "Michael, I'd really like to get to know you better." That's all it took. He immediately asked me out for a drink. We've been together now for four and a half years.*
> **Teri (age 43) talking about Michael (age 28)**

Always give him the option to make the first move, but help him in small ways. A longer than normal gaze or a smile that is warm and welcoming can be all you need. Make sure that you are alone, not in the company of friends or other people, so that he can approach you more comfortably. If these methods are too subtle, yet you are otherwise confident that he is very definitely attracted to you, we offer some examples of ways in which you can gently encourage him.

Our friend Gail met her boyfriend of five years at a local soup kitchen where they both volunteered their time to help feed the homeless. They would see each other every Sunday and became quite friendly as they worked together, telling each other about their lives. She knew that they had a strong mutual attraction, but, given their seventeen-year age difference, she knew that he lacked the courage to come right out and ask her for a date. He'd been talking about how demanding his job was so she made a little joke out of it. "With those long hours, how will you ever find time to go to a movie with me?" she asked him playfully. It did the trick.

Sandra, age forty-one, had been having ongoing, lengthy conversations with Erik, age twenty-seven, in her gym. They were both fitness buffs, so this was a place where they saw each other on a regular basis and were able to engage in discussions about their mutual interests which, besides health and physical fitness, included self-improvement and spirituality. After several months, Sandra mentioned to Erik that she had found a fabulous church which she was now attending. Erik said he'd love to go sometime. She invited him for the following Sunday and they have now been together for over six years. He didn't exactly ask her out (nor she him). He asked to join her, which was his way of protecting his ego. The result was the same. Of course he needed her phone number in case there was a problem...you know the rest.

Helping him make the first move is one thing. Making that move your-self is something else and we do not recommend it. Don't ask him out. You can offer him the rope, but if he doesn't grab it there's a reason. Consider that it's just not meant to be and let it go.

Do not ask men out. Simply make it easier for them to ask you. Most of the younger men we've interviewed said that they couldn't believe their older woman would ever consider going out with them.

> *Go out with me? Are you kidding? I was amazed that she would even want to talk to me. She looked like she had everything—an interesting life, you know?—so I thought she was just being polite. No, I don't think I would have had the nerve to ask her out. She was the one who offered to introduce me to someone she knew who was into collecting the sports cards I was thinking about selling. She even took me to meet the guy and then I was able to invite her out for dinner to celebrate the sale. That's how we started and, to tell you the truth, I'm still amazed!*
>
> **Ollie (age 31)**

The young men were sure the women had many older, more powerful men swarming around them. They couldn't believe their good fortune when they realized the women were interested in them as well. That was the reason for their delay. These men so enjoyed being with and talking to these women, they didn't want to blow it. So they settled for brief conver-sations rather than risking a move that might lose them altogether. So be kind to him, be gentle with him, but be firm. Make it okay for him to be a man. Lead him to where he really wants to go. He will be grateful that you did.

Chapter 16

Designing the Relationship

It wouldn't have worked for me years ago,
but at this point in my life, it's absolutely perfect.
Martha (age 56)

A ten-year or more age difference raises issues about the degree to which a couple chooses to merge their lives. When a forty-year-old man becomes involved with a twenty-year-old girl, he is almost forced to marry her because of the extreme social censure he would face if he didn't. He, as the one with the power, experience and (most likely) the money, would be seen as taking advantage of her innocence and vulnerability if he didn't marry her and take care of her. He would pretty much have to provide her with a home and a general sense that her security was in his capable and responsible hands.

How Close Do You Want to Be?
The same standard, however, doesn't hold true when an older woman and a younger man couple. Men are not perceived as innocent or vulnerable, and nobody expects that their wives or girlfriends take care of them. They are perfectly capable of fending for themselves and this fact liberates women in a number of ways. First of all, as we've said before, marriage may or may not be the option of choice for you. Maybe you'll want to get married. If so, fine. Do it and enjoy the blessings. Maybe you just want to live together. That's fine, too. Maybe you'd rather live apart and get together several times a week. Maybe he stays in his own home during the week and spends weekends with you. Your options are varied and they are numerous. You are breaking new ground in more than one way.

Astrid, age sixty-one, and Renaldo, age forty-seven, have been a monoga-mous, committed couple for thirteen years, but they've never lived together. Both say that they enjoy having their own space. They generally spend no more than four nights a week together, mostly at Astrid's home, although occasionally, when she wants a change of scenery, they stay at Renaldo's. "It keeps things fresh, like the beginning of a relationship...we never get bored or sick of seeing each other. It works for us."

Together, the two of you are free to design the relationship according to your needs and desires. The choices are numerous and they are yours to make.

Karolina, a lovely Swedish woman of eighty, lives with her companion of twenty-five years, Paolo, who is sixteen years her junior. They met when she was in her fifties. Being European, the need to marry didn't hold the importance that it did in the United States. They have chosen a permanent relationship of living together, partially because Karolina would stand to lose her former husband's sizable pension were she to remarry. This has worked wonderfully for them and hasn't diminished or devalued their part-nership. Marriage, in their case, wouldn't mean that they are more com-mitted or more in love. Their living arrangement is merely one that works well for them.

Another couple we interviewed decided that marriage was the best choice for them. Carl was sixteen years younger than Pam and wanted to be fully engaged in the lives of her children. They were concerned that Carl would be viewed as "mom's boyfriend" and subtly excluded from the chil-dren's school and social events. Carl was eager to unify his new family and wanted to fully take on the responsibility and role of being the children's "dad." Living in a midwestern suburb, both Pam and Carl felt the children needed stability to have a common ground with other children in their school and community. In their case, as Pam relates, these factors played a major role in their decision-making process:

> I didn't want Carl to be left out. Ashley was having some problems with math and I was scheduled to have a meeting with her teacher. Carl wanted to be there, but as my "boyfriend" he wouldn't have been taken as seriously. He is such a part of their lives, and the thought of excluding him because he was viewed as "only a boyfriend" was something we didn't want to live with.

Exercising these kinds of choices in accordance with your needs makes sense for various reasons. When an older woman becomes involved with a man ten or more years younger than herself, it's likely that she has more money, more sophistication and more experience than he does. The two may have significantly different interests. Can you imagine being an opera buff and trying to drag your young hard-rock-loving mate to the local opera house? Telling him how he should dress for the occasion? Watching him squirm through what might be for him a miserable evening, just because he wants to please you? Who needs it? You not only don't have to live together, you also don't have to do everything together. Go and enjoy the opera with one of your friends who shares your passion for it. Let him go out and pursue his interests. Savor your times together by doing only those things that you both enjoy.

> *I was in my fifties when I met Dan. I was divorced and living alone after my kids moved out. It was heaven. I had no one to clean up after and only my own laundry to do. It was great. Dan was thirty-seven and we got along beautifully. He moved in with me, but it was a disaster. He's a creature who's comfortable with chaos, but I'm not. He would constantly make a mess and I would constantly run around cleaning it up. Even when he tried to do better, his idea of clean was light years away from mine. He was kind of immature in other ways, too. If I had met him thirty years earlier, I'd like to think that I would have had enough brains not to marry him! Anyway, our relationship was deteriorating and I asked him to move out. But we loved each other and neither one of us wanted to end the relationship. So now he lives in his own (hideously disorganized) apartment and I live in my house. He comes over a couple of nights a week and we have a wonderful time together. He may be immature and messy, but he's also loving and devoted and a really good person. I'm very happy with things just the way they are. He is, too. What can I tell you? It wouldn't have worked for me years ago when I was raising a family, but at this point in my life, it's absolutely perfect.*
>
> **Martha (age 56)**

Suppose you are a high-earning professional woman and the man of your dreams does construction work. Are you comfortable introducing him to your circle of friends and colleagues? If you are, then you are a secure person and comfortable with yourself. But if this makes you uncomfortable, that's okay, too. You don't have to bring him to cocktail parties or the office holiday gala. You are free to design this relationship and every aspect of it to suit your needs. Do what feels right for you. Don't feel that you have to conform to some old social models that say "this, and only this" is what loving, committed relationships look like. The power of choice is a heady one. Go ahead and use it to your heart's content. Both you and your younger man will appreciate it and be happier because you have.

Chapter 17

His Friends/ Her Friends

What would my friends think, me carrying on with a guy so young?
Joanne (age 42)

When you and your significantly younger man are alone together, you will probably both tend to concentrate on common interests and experiences. The differences in interests, musical taste and personal style are not so glaring and often don't seem to matter very much. You are aware that differences exist, but so what? They can be endearing and humorous and you can both laugh about them. However, when you find yourself surrounded by people in his age group or he's enmeshed in a group of people in your age category, it's a different story and can be a very uncomfortable experience. Suddenly you realize that they are speaking a different language, one that you've never learned, or perhaps references to past events are being made in a conversation and he is clueless because it all happened when he was still very young. Bridging one decade is not so difficult, but beyond that you may find yourself immersed in an entirely different culture.

Lynda, age forty-seven, was socializing with twenty-eight-year-old Keith and his friends at an outdoor barbecue. The music was foreign to her, the slang and contemporary expressions were foreign to her, as was the overall group consciousness. She felt totally alone, not to mention hyper aware of her age. She commented that someone she knew was an "Archie Bunker" type. Nobody knew what she meant. Talking about music later that same day, she remarked that she loved the old Motown sound. There was deafening silence. It was obvious that nobody knew what she was talking about. End of conversation.

Usually, when your younger guy is with you, he makes every effort to come up to your level. The two of you develop your own form of communication. What had initially brought you together is keeping you together now. But when he is with his peers, the differences between you seem multiplied exponentially.

I don't know what it is about guys when they get together, but they seem to regress. I watched Bill, who is levelheaded and mature when he's with me, become about twelve or thirteen with his friends. They were spouting off one-liners from movies they saw and doing character imitations, making weird noises—it was a trip! Fortunately, one of the gals in the group was interesting. She was a physical therapist and with my medical background we had a lot to talk about. I ended up talking to her the whole night.

Gail (age 42)

In some instances, seeing your younger man with his friends and observing his behavior among them can serve to snap you out of infatuation and into a more realistic assessment of the man with whom you're dealing.

His friends were idiots. Total morons, and I use the word clinically. Immature oafs, just incredibly dumb. And so was he, really. It's just that I must have been so blinded by the sexual chemistry that I closed my eyes to it. It was only after I saw him with his friends and realized how idiotic and juvenile they were that I was able to see how inadequate he was. There I was, forty-five-years-old and in heat for what? A pair of biceps? I realized then that I had to end it. It couldn't possibly have a future. Let me tell you, it was a really rude awakening.

Alicia (age 51)

What to do? It's been our observation that typically there will be at least one person or one couple in his sphere with whom you can communicate and whom you will enjoy. Somewhere among his group of friends there will be those individuals who, for whatever reason, have a broader knowledge and a more mature view of the world. They may be rare, but they probably exist and with them you will surely find a greater comfort level. Your job is to seek them out. This requires that you initiate the effort to engage his friends in conversation. While much of this effort may be fruitless and perhaps even somewhat uncomfortable for you, it will make your guy happy to see you reaching out to his group. And when you do find those people with whom you can relate, it will make being with his friends a lot less of a chore. You might even begin to enjoy it. Here are some additional tips:

- If you are terribly uncomfortable with his small, more intimate circle, try to only go to larger gatherings with him. There you will increase your chances of finding people with whom you can communicate and feel more at ease.

- Pick and choose events and people carefully. Some activities only accentuate the differences between you. If he wants to go to a certain type of concert and you're really not into the scene, don't go. You won't make him happy or yourself happy. You'll both have a better time doing your own things.

- Take evenings apart from one another to socialize with your own friends. You don't need to be joined at the hip, any more than a "same-age" couple needs to do everything together.

- Look for new areas of interest that both of you can share. Rock climbing, jazz concerts, nature hikes, flea markets or museums might fit the bill. Remember that younger men tend to be a lot more open to doing new and different things. They are not yet overly set in their ways. Their minds haven't locked into "Oh no, I don't do that." They are still interested in discovering the many facets of life and will surprise you with their adventurous attitude. Take full advantage of this; it's an opportunity to develop a new set of mutual friends with whom you can both relate easily.

Outside of establishing new friends as a couple, when you are with his peers stay open-minded and flexible. You are in the relationship to grow, too. It's not just about him learning to adapt to your lifestyle. You will be exposed to new interests, a new language, different points of view, new musical styles. That's great. You have the opportunity to acquire more depth and a broader dimension to yourself. You develop some idea of what the thoughts, attitudes and behaviors of another generation are about. As a result, you'll probably have a lot more in common with your own children or with your nieces and nephews. Your newfound knowledge can enrich these relationships as well.

Your choice to be with a much younger man has catapulted you into a new zone of freedom and liberation. If your relationship endures, you will inevitably be forced to grow, to expand your horizons and to become more flexible. It is the best way to stay youthful, vibrant and in touch with emerging generations.

When I look at pictures of myself from five years ago, I can't believe it's me—corporate look, controlled hairstyles, out of shape, wearing long, frumpy skirts. Looking at those pictures makes me realize what an impact Irwin has had on my life. I didn't ever consciously "try" to change; I felt okay about myself. Obviously his energy and youth had an effect on me. I think I just began to change inside. I know I felt freer and more alive. I lightened my hair and started wearing less of the man-tailored things I was used to, opting instead for romantic dresses. I didn't even try to lose weight, but he was so active and I got into things I never imagined I'd be interested in. Five years ago if you had told me I'd be rollerblading, I would have suggested you see a psychiatrist, but here I am...

Mary (age 53)

His Friends

- When beginning to meet his friends, remember to start small. For both of you, one friend at a time is a lot less threatening than a group. Pick his most supportive and compassionate friend with whom to develop a relationship. Start there and expand outward.

- Make the first meetings with his friends brief and casual. Both of you should have the opportunity to leave should the situation become too uncomfortable. Instead of inviting his friend (whom you've never met) over for dinner, where you're stuck with each other for the evening, suggest that you stop by to say hello the next time he and your boyfriend are having a drink.

- The first time the two of you go to a larger group function, make sure it's one where his "supportive friend" is present. That gives you both a feeling of security and someone you can talk to. We know that at your age and with your level of life experience you can handle any crowd. However, handling a situation and feeling comfortable are two entirely different things.

- Find a common thread. Whether it's golf, tennis or a great movie you all want to see, these types of shared activities can ease the social tension. When you're engaged in a group activity, the one-on-one conversation isn't so important.

- Don't force yourself on his crowd or try too hard to be accepted. As with any other random group of people, some will like you and some won't. That's okay. It's natural. Be yourself. Be real. Be open. Ask questions about their lives and areas of interest. They'll be flattered and will have something to talk about. You might even learn something.

Your Friends

Your friends are, hopefully, on your side. If they really love you and want you to be happy, they will be supportive.

Thank God for Cathy. I was feeling so embarrassed. What would my friends think, me carrying on with a guy so young? I was ashamed, judging myself and projecting that judgment onto my friends. But Cathy, bless her heart, just looked at him and said to me, "What a dreamboat. How did you get so lucky?" I immediately relaxed and felt good about Ray and me.

Joanne (age 42)

Sometimes, however, our friends are not supportive. They don't get it or they are offended by it. One woman we spoke with, Ruth, told us that she'd had a girlfriend, Marsha, who was particularly critical and scornful. She was always harping on why it was so inappropriate for Ruth to be with someone so young. Ruth had to break off the friendship with Marsha because she couldn't handle the constant put-downs any longer. Three years later she saw Marsha again, only now Marsha was head over heels in love and living with her new boyfriend, a fellow fourteen years younger. Sometimes it's just about timing. One day a person isn't ready for it and two days later they change. Timing can be everything.

Other times it's simply about that old green-eyed monster, jealousy. Another friend of ours, Rita, found herself unexpectedly involved with a younger man she had met in her office. Rita, though in her so-called middle years, is quite good looking and in great physical shape. Of course she works at it by going to the gym daily, watching what she eats, not smoking—and it shows. She looks terrific. But despite the fact that both she and her younger man were single adults, their liaison was being compared by some of their co-workers to another office romance involving two people who were married and cheating on their respective spouses. Rita shared with us a note she had received from one of her "concerned" co-workers:

It's been pointed out to me that you and Miguel had surprisingly similar weekends—canoeing in the rain, etc. And you're both wearing the same wristbands today. As your friend, Rita, I just wanted to point that out to you. THIS IS NOT A JUDGMENT AT ALL. I have absolutely no opinion whatsoever. I am not jumping to conclusions, nor would I ever. I am your friend and simply wish someone as worthy, lovely and truly kind as you to never tread the same ground as the likes of [Here she inserted the names of the adulterous couple.] I hope to dear God I have not offended you. It's not easy to come up with this, but I want to try to protect you a little, in case you might need it.

Very lovingly, Jean

The writer of this note happened to be an unhappy young woman who had no love life of her own to speak of. Sometimes we must, unfortunately, consider where some of our "dear friends" are really coming from. It may not necessarily be our best interest that motivates them.

The First Meeting

Upon introducing your younger man to your friends, again start slowly. Don't bring him to meet your whole crowd at once. He'll feel like he's on display.

> *I met some of her girlfriends and I felt very uncomfortable because of some giggles and some comments they made. I thought they were coming on to me a little bit. I don't know. I felt that they were curious, that they wanted to know what was going on and what the story was. It made me feel funny, like they thought I was her puppet.*

Alex (age 39)

To avoid making your younger man go through what Alex experienced, there are some things you should keep in mind:

■ Start with one close female friend. Make it a casual meeting, allowing both to feel free to exit if they so desire. Meet her for coffee or a drink in a place where he already feels comfortable. Keep it light and fun; no big interviews, please. He will tell you how he felt about her. Hopefully, she liked him. By letting them both start off slowly, they can warm up to each other.

■ Wait awhile before you bring him into a larger circle and, when you do, make sure it is something he will enjoy attending. The best activity is one where he can come and go as he pleases. Difficulties can arise if he finds himself in a position of having to be somebody he's not. A Sunday night buffet at an exclusive country club can be difficult for anyone new to that scene. If he's feeling stressed, he'll make less of a good impression.

Although he's not in the same age group as your friends, they may still share some common ground. The older he is, the less of an issue this becomes. Try to expose him to those of your friends he might relate to best. Trust that he will eventually find some friends among your social circle. Keep him in mind when scheduling events. The more he is exposed to your group, the greater his comfort level and yours. Remember, not everyone's same-aged partner is social or active in his wife's or girlfriend's circle.

Don't expect him to jump through hoops. If he's wonderful in your eyes, he's bound to be wonderful in some of your friends' eyes as well.

Chapter 18

Social Functions: When to Include/ When to Exclude

An older man I knew whispered to me, "Why in the world would you bring your toy here?" I wanted to die.
Denise (age 43)

If your younger man is not living with you, the question of including or excluding him in your social plans need not be a problem. If there is a social function coming up and there is any doubt in your mind about the advisability of bringing him along—go alone. Bring him only to those functions that are appropriate, comfortable and fun for both of you.

In a committed, live-in relationship, a younger man can feel rejected if you exclude him from an important social event. You would feel rejected, too, if the situation were reversed. However, his fear might be that you are ashamed of him, that he isn't good enough or doesn't make the grade with your crowd. Especially if there is a significant socio-economic difference between you, you may both feel uncomfortable. Say you have a black-tie affair—and he's never worn a tuxedo. Do you rent one for him? Do you even take him?

If you really want him to go to the event with you and it's important that he be there, then go ahead. Bring him. Have him rent or buy a tuxedo. Actually, it could be a fun experience for both of you. Remember the scene in the film *Titanic* in which Leonardo DiCaprio is invited to the first class dining room? He seemed transformed into an elegant gentleman once he donned the borrowed tuxedo. Clothes do influence the way we walk, talk and feel about ourselves. Our demeanor in high heels and a gorgeous gown is infused with grace and elegance—a totally different feeling than when we are clad in leggings and a sweater. It might be wonderful to share his first black-tie event. An elegant evening for both of you can be very romantic. Things to think about when making this decision are contingent upon your younger guy's style, charisma and social graces. Don't be too harsh when he whines about the discomfort he feels in formal clothes. We guarantee there will be countless stiff, awkward, uncomfortable older gentlemen in the crowd that evening who also can't wait to retreat homeward and tear off their "monkey suits" as soon as possible.

To help you decide whether to include or exclude him the next time you plan to attend an event or social obligation, here are some things you might consider:

- Estimate if it's worth him feeling uncomfortable and possibly you feeling uncomfortable as well. How will that impact your relationships with the other guests? This calls for discernment on your part. If not thoughtfully considered in advance, an error in judgment could lead to a big blow-up later on between you and your mate.

I really wanted to take Rick to my friend's wedding reception. I thought he'd love the elegance of her powerful and affluent crowd. But he was really uncomfortable. It was agony for both of us. He didn't have anything in common with the couples at our table—he became reactive and defensive. It made everything worse. I was so embarrassed—I had to do damage control the whole evening. An older man I knew whispered to me, "Why in the world would you bring your toy here?" I wanted to die. Thank God the bride was a very close friend—she was sympathetic, but I'd never do that again. It was way outside of Rick's comfort level.

Denise (age 43)

- Determine if he truly wants to go or if he is trying to please you. If he has any reservations, let him stay home. He should not feel pressured into entering what he may consider a hostile or unpleasant environment. Respect his decision. He is not a child. Don't treat him like one!

Jenny had this office party and she wanted me to go. I don't like the whole "suit" thing...but then I was thinking, I'm with her, so I should go. I just couldn't see myself standing there all night being introduced to a bunch of people I'd never see again. We fought about it all week. It became this big deal and it was only a party.

Patrick (age 27)

■ Are there advantages for both of you? Could he possibly get a better view of your world and would that help to widen the parameters of your social life together? Could this be an introduction to a new event or area of interest, as well as exposure to new friends, that you can share together?

I was invited to a celebrity golf tournament followed by a black-tie dinner. Tom and I had met on a golf course so he was thrilled. The day went great as we followed the players over the course and at the dinner later he was in heaven talking golf all evening. He just meshed well with everyone there. When it comes to golf, these people can talk for hours and he was in his element even though he'd never worn a tuxedo before.

Melissa (age 39)

Introducing Him

How do you introduce him? If the relationship is new and you are bringing him out to meet your friends and co-workers, finding the right label that appropriately says what he is, without diminishing either one of you, can be challenging. Don't offend him or yourself. Lovers hate to be introduced as "my friend." It's a slap in the face. Better yet, say simply, "This is Tom" or "This is my date, Tom." After the relationship has solidified, and you are a definite couple, possible choices might be "partner," "mate" or "boyfriend." Even in a casual relationship, don't use the word "lover." It may be true. Maybe that's all he is to you, but be a lady and give the relationship a sense of significance whenever possible.

How you introduce him can be crucial to your relationship. Make him feel important and comfortable. You would want him to do the same for you. How you show your respect for him in social situations will influence how others will respect him and his existence in your life.

Your Choices

What about you attending functions that involve his circle of friends? All sorts of unexpected issues—and misunderstandings—can arise. Stephanie, age thirty-eight, and Robert, age twenty-three, were very much in love, but it was a relatively new relationship and they were still learning how to communicate with each other. Robert's band was giving a concert and he strongly dissuaded Stephanie from attending. She felt hurt, confused and excluded. Calling her best friend, Helen, for consolation made her feel even worse. Helen's take on the situation was that Robert loved having sex with her in private, but was ashamed of her in public. Helen insisted that Robert had a groupie girlfriend or two and that Stephanie's presence at the event would ruin his plans. Stephanie decided to show up anyway and, to her surprise, was greeted with open arms. Robert proudly introduced her as his girlfriend to everyone. Later he explained that it was *he* who was embarrassed because his alternative/punk style band catered to a "kiddie" audience and he didn't want *her* to think less of him, as she was so sophisticated and cultured. They are still together today.

Even well-meaning friends may not see the whole picture. If they don't know him, they may assume the worst. They've been conditioned to do that by all of the old stereotypes and false beliefs about older women/younger men relationships. Only when they really get to know him can they make an accurate assessment of his character. Always search your heart. You are the one who knows him best.

Think twice, however, about attending functions at which you will be out of place and uncomfortable. You might be madly in love with him, but spending a long evening with a group of people with whom you have almost nothing in common can be difficult.

> Not only were his friends from school all getting married, but his sisters and all his cousins were, too. And they were having—or talking about having—babies. I'm so far beyond that point in my life that I just couldn't relate. My smile was frozen on my face and I was bored to tears. I never want to go to another wedding in my life. At least not for the thirty-something crowd.
>
> **Peggy (age 49)**

> My husband's family is "social register" and my first introduction to them was at their yacht club. It was hard enough to be on display as "his older girlfriend," but to be thrown into that type of setting with so many people was unbearable.
>
> The conversation focused on three topics: sailing (which I don't do), foreign cities (that I have never seen) and their inner circle of friends (whom I don't know). I had nothing to say all night and they never asked me about myself.
>
> **Cynthia (age 48)**

Regarding inclusion/exclusion at social gatherings, apply the same type of thinking for your treatment of him to his treatment of you:

- Has he invited you to a function you will enjoy? Even though it's different, could the new experience be fun?
- Do you feel you "should go" simply because you *are* his partner?
- Is the cost of the discomfort one you can afford to pay?
- Is there a worse-case scenario if you don't attend?

- Is there an alternative choice? Arriving alone later? Leaving together earlier? Agreeing only to stay an hour or two?
- Is there a benefit/gain possible by attending? Could you go with an open mind and possibly learn something new?

There are people who assume because they are "a couple" they need to attend every social function together. Perhaps the thinking is "If we don't go together, our relationship will deteriorate" or "Since we are a couple, we need to show a united front."

If obligation is combined with a sense of self-imposed duty or guilt, you have a recipe for disaster. If you both *want* to be there, fine. If one of you doesn't want to attend, then that should be fine too. Being a couple doesn't mean being Siamese twins.

In evaluating the pros and cons of attendance at social functions, we suggest you hear out your partner's concerns and communicate your own as well. Good relationships often mean meeting somewhere in the middle—trying to find a way in which both partners can participate and make the occasion a win-win situation.

Chapter 19

Handling
His Family

You lucky bastard! How in the world did you ever get a woman like that?
Mort (age 53), father of Fred (age 28)

Whenever two people decide to become a couple, they sooner or later realize they are not the only people involved in the relationship. Parents, children, siblings and other family members enter the picture, becoming a part of the fabric of the couple's life. Sometimes this is a blessing and other times it is not.

While judgment and social censure from friends and acquaintances often accompany the union of an older woman and a younger man, the greatest degree of anger and discrimination will usually come from within his family and, more specifically, from his mother. Generally, this is a problem for younger men even if they are ready, willing and able to commit to a relationship with a woman. Of course, the older a man is when he enters this relationship, the greater (we hope) is the degree to which he has separated from his mother and adopted his own identity, thoughts and lifestyle. He is then better equipped to withstand her resistance. However, there are certainly some men—of all ages—who never move out from under their mothers' thumbs.

Even in the healthiest, most understanding family, the younger man's mother will likely be concerned and hesitant at first about the age difference between you. Fathers, oddly, don't generally share this concern or at least do so to much lesser degrees. Many of our couples reported mixed reactions from members of the younger man's family. The good news is that as unions between older women and younger men become more prevalent, the acceptance of these relationships grows. However, you must deal with the here and now. We hope to make what can be difficult for you easier.

His mother hated me...his father tolerated me, because he felt that the contribution I made to the relationship was beneficial, and his younger brother liked me for who I was.

Alana (age 58)

There were mixed emotions from my family, which stemmed from a true concern for my well-being. Much, if not all, of the bad reactions dissipated after the family had seen us together and had gotten to know and admire her.

Al (age 27)

Most mothers of younger men will feel protective of their sons' interests at first. His mother probably won't understand what you see in him and will be suspicious of your intentions. If she can respond without hysteria, she will most likely adopt a wait-and-see attitude. Expect a "trial period" during which his mother determines for herself who you are and whether you are bringing pain or joy into her son's life. The best case scenario is one in which his mother does—in time—get over her own idea of what is best for him and loves and accepts you, because you so obviously make him happy.

I could see that Sheila and Matt worked well together. They invited my husband and me over for Thanksgiving; they were so excited to have us over in their new apartment. I saw their closeness. It was like they were a team. And while I never thought it would turn out this way, Matt with an older woman, I know they are very happy. I love my son and I just want him to be happy. If Sheila does that for him, it's good enough for me.

Matilda (age 51)

We were both (my husband and I) very concerned at first that our son had fallen in love with an older woman. But I had heard she was a wonderful person from other people I knew. It was a shock...not something we ever expected. I decided to just wait and see—I couldn't stand the thought of him being hurt, but I didn't know what else to do. He had to find out for himself. Now she is a part of our family and we really do love her. I don't even think of her as older anymore. She's just Karen—and my son loves her.

Helen (age 45)

Sometimes the initial concern and hesitation, even resistance, to the relationship from his mother grows into acceptance and tolerant resignation.

She's not what I would have chosen for him, but it was different years ago. Women didn't want young men, they wanted older men. Certainly, I never knew a man who sought older women, but I guess it's whatever they really want that counts. I'd like grandchildren and I'm not sure that's going to happen. But it's got to be what he wants and I can't make those decisions for him. It's hard for me at times. I guess that's just being a "mom."

Phyllis (age 56)

Well, at least we can go through menopause together.

Linda (age 49)

We also discovered many cases of happy acceptance from his family, often because they recognized what good influences the older women were on the younger men's lives. Here are a number of examples:

What amazed me was Kevin's family. I was very concerned, to say the least, about meeting them. It turns out they are the most wonderful, warm, loving people I have ever met. And it's sincere; it's not hypocritical. He had already told them about our relationship before I met them, so they had time to adjust to the idea. Now his mother sends me articles and gifts and she always signs the cards, "Mother."

Josepha (age 54)

My dad was envious and my mother was concerned. I mean, I was twenty-two and she was thirty-six, beautiful and successful. They didn't get it. My cousin Jim told me, "Thank you for showing me that my childhood fantasies can come true." After a little while, everyone in the family, even my grandmother, accepted it. They really grew to love her.

Calvin (age 25)

My family didn't know for a long time and they were a little shocked, to say the least. They weren't surprised by who she was, but her age, when it came out, gave them a jolt. It wasn't like a negative or positive reaction, just surprise. They thought she was a great person. They didn't suspect she was thirty-eight, because she didn't look her age. So the subject of age never came up. When it finally did though, they were very cool about it.

Mike (age 27)

I met Oliver's mother many years ago when he asked her to see me. He was still quite young, in his early twenties. She thought I was wonderful. She could not believe the good effect I had on her son. She loved me, she thought I was wonderful. I told her that he was really in love with me and she suggested we have an affair! I told her it was already underway and she thought that was marvelous, too.

Penny (Age 62)

David came from a very religious, very conservative and traditional family. I didn't know how they would take to me. I was really nervous, scared and a little intimidated. I had played out every type of reaction I could think of so I'd be prepared for anything. They were a little quiet at first, then slowly, as the night wore on, they got more open and talkative. We discovered we had a lot of things in common and I was feeling better. They were really quite gracious. I know it's nothing they ever imagined they would have to deal with, but they have turned out to be loving and supportive. I really feel like a part of his family now.

Arlene (age 47)

His mom was eight years older than I. She was a single parent of four children. Another of her sons was living with a woman the same age as me (thirteen-year age difference). She told her third son to find a thirty-eight-year-old woman, too. She felt I was a "good catch."

Ellen (age 39)

Mark's parents said, "Go for it. If you can grab some happiness in this life, you should."

Patricia (age 51)

His mother took me aside and had a conversation with me. I felt that she just wanted to know my intentions. I promised her that no matter how long we were together, three months, three years or thirty years, I would do everything in my power to make him happy. I said I loved him and really wanted the best for him and that I had never had a relationship to date where I took away a man's self-esteem or abused his loving nature. I knew his mother and I connected at that moment. And she knew I was for real. I kept my word and his whole family treats me with love and respect.

Susan (age 44)

You may not be what his family expected him to bring home and you may not have been their choice as his mate, but a family who truly is invested in their son's happiness will see the benefits and happiness you bring to his life. Give them time to get to know you. Don't try too hard. Be yourself and be real. After all, they raised him to be the man you fell in love with so they must have some of the qualities you love in him.

Expect a normal warming-up period. Many families have never been exposed to this type of relationship before. It may take a little time for them to see you for what you are, but be patient. This is new to them. They are just beginning to see in you what he has already seen and come to love.

Remember that the age difference, because it is the gender reverse of what is considered socially acceptable, makes you a target for criticism. Don't go out of your way to court more. Don't push anyone to accept your relationship. Don't force invitations to his family functions. Work out a game plan with your partner as to who goes where, with whom and on which holidays. Steer clear of family members who feel entitled to be abusive, hostile or threatening no matter how righteous they think their indignation is.

Expect family members' reactions to run a gamut of emotions, especially in the beginning. Remember, however, that this is your life and, unless you have young children, you should focus on your and your mate's happiness. Keep in mind that other people's reactions are an expression of their fears, doubts, biases and belief systems and that none of these necessarily reflect your reality. If you and your young man are comfortable with each other and treat each other with love and respect, his family and yours will be influenced by that eventually. The people who love you will want you both to be happy.

The Talk

However mixed or even seemingly positive his family's reactions to you are, be prepared for "The Talk." This is a legendary rite of passage more commonly experienced by a young man upon his introduction to a young woman's family. It is taken to new heights, however, when the prospective partner of a young man is an older woman. As an older woman involved with a much younger man, you may be considered by some people to be a vulture-like, manipulative seductress out to control and dominate him. Your age makes you an easy target. The relationship of a same age couple may contain all sorts of negatives like addiction, abuse or infidelity, but these can be hidden from onlookers. Age, like race, makes your differences highly visible. You can be the most wonderful person with nothing but good to offer a young man, but your age makes you an easy target for interference and criticism from the member of his family who is most threatened by you.

If there is going to be a problem, it usually is going to come from the women in his life, either his mother or, in some cases, his sister(s). In most cases, it is his mother who precipitates "The Talk."

Expect "The Talk" to take place when she realizes that you are not some fly-by-night fling, but a serious contender for her son's affections. It may come (and often does) the first time you meet her or at the first holiday or other family gathering you attend. "The Talk" must happen quickly, because she isn't sure she'll have the opportunity to see you again. Although we refer to it as "The Talk," it is really a question: "What do you want with him?" In most instances, his mother genuinely loves and only wants to protect her "baby."

For many women, dating a younger man is just dating a younger man. We cannot understand the anxiety and confusion this can strike in his mother. It is important to be sensitive to her concern for her son, to let her know you are not just playing with him and that your intention is to enrich his life not take away from it. However, if his mother is invested in being the primary woman in his life (and she has turned her son into an "emotional husband") she may be frightened, angry and dangerous. In that case, nothing you say will placate her.

"The Talk" will let you know, either directly or indirectly, if she has grave doubts about you and about the quality of your relationship. She might say: "My real concern is that men like my son are very easily influenced and I know you play a big part in his life."

- or -

"I just don't think it's right. You cannot possibly make this work. I want him to have a normal life."

- or -

"My son and I are very close. I want him to be happy..." (Implying, of course, that you will come between them *and* make him miserable.)

Under whatever circumstances you find yourself confronted with "The Talk," don't panic and don't get angry. Begin your response by giving his mother the reassurance she needs. Here's how one woman we know, Lily, handled the conversation:

I know my history in relationships. I can promise you, as I sit here now, I will add to the quality of your son's life. Where he is today and where he will be, if the time comes that we need to part, I promise you he will be in a better place. He will be more self-confident and filled with more self-love and he will have gained from his time spent with me.

Allow his mother to get to know you through your demeanor and responses. The relationship between you and her son is not quite what she envisioned for him so she has to thoroughly check you out. She wants to know what to expect, so be honest, direct and truthful. Here are some tips:

■ **Only Answer Appropriate Questions**
This is not the time to tell her about your abusive and alcoholic ex-husband or your years in therapy finding out who you really are. She's not a friend—yet. She's trying to put the pieces of the puzzle together. Hold your own, but in a pleasant manner. Be forthcoming, but not too revealing about your own issues. Giving out too much information could provide her with ammunition to use against you later. The less said the better.

■ **Be Nice**
Be warm, genuine and direct. Address any misconceptions she may have. You may choose to tell her your values or simply acknowledge

that you have registered and understand her concerns. Don't make promises you can't keep. Don't let her talk you out of the relationship. Let her know that your intentions are also focused on his well-being.

■ **Let Her Talk**
She simply may need to vocalize some of her fears and projections. When people get a chance to be heard, they often feel that a connection has been established between themselves and the listener. Allowing her to state her concerns will enable you to become aware of her "triggers"—her big issues concerning her son's new relationship.

■ **Try to Create an Alliance**
Let her know that you and she are united in your desire to see him happy. You are, after all, the two women who care about him the most. Be aware, however, that this may not always be possible. Where she's going with this discussion is unpredictable. She could be simply taking your measure or it could end with her expressing her total disapproval and telling you to get out of his life.

■ **Know Where Your Younger Man Stands**
Is he willing to stand up to his mother if push comes to shove? Many a young man simply assumes that of course his mother will love you— just because he thinks you're so great. He won't know her true emotions and attitudes until after he's introduced you to her as someone special in his life. So talk to him about it in advance. Ask him what he would do if she doesn't like you or won't accept the relationship. Ask him directly: "What would you do? Would you leave the relationship if she doesn't approve?" There is no use getting armed for a battle and then discovering you are fighting alone.

■ **Be Wary of Ongoing Discussion**
If, after the first discussion, his mother still needs to talk about it again, you could be in trouble. Her need to keep getting back into the issue is usually a sign that she's not able to let go and accept her son's choice of a mate. Several women told us about numerous late night phone calls during which the mothers "just had to clear something up" or "needed to talk about it." A mother like this is, and may remain, too involved. Remind her that you and her son *both* want to be together.

One woman we know, Diana, thought "The Talk" went very well, only to discover her younger man becoming more distant and detached. It finally clicked when she heard him express several of his mother's fear-based pro-jections (repeated in his mother's exact words). The man wasn't mature enough to separate his concerns from those of his mother. He took on her fears without filtering them through his own feelings. Diana called him on it. At first, he was highly defensive and denied that he was mouthing his mother's thoughts. Later, however, he admitted that they had "talked about it a lot lately." He was still heavily invested in making his mother happy first and not in having a mature relationship.

Some (very) young men have only had one woman in their lives...*their mom*. This makes her a very powerful figure. If you sense a sudden rift, it could be his mother getting him aside and "repositioning" his mind. He has to be strong enough and clear enough about wanting to be with you and willing to take a stand that puts him squarely at your side. One woman dis-covered her young man was playing both sides of the fence to keep the love and approval of the two major females in his life. He would agree with his mother on the fact that it couldn't last, then tell his girlfriend he was deeply committed to her. Such ambivalence won't do. This man was simply too immature and too weak to be truthful (if he even knew his own feelings). Get the game plan set with him first. It could save you a lot of heartache.

- **Give It Time**

  In time you will know everything you need to know about his mother as well as him. How he responds to his mother can serve as either a unifying force between you and your younger man or the beginning of your discovery that he's just too young.

- **Don't Badmouth Her**

  A son can say whatever negative things he wants to about his parents, but you must not. Give his mother time to accept your relationship. When you are clear about her position—and his—speak up, expressing your perspective. Be tactful, but be truthful. It is crucial that you com-municate openly with your guy, but trying to turn him against his mother will only backfire and hurt you in the end. He has a long-standing allegiance to her, which you must respect. Let him know that her disapproval hurts you, but avoid negativity and name-calling. We guarantee that he'll remember the unkind things you said about her and it will do more to alienate his affection from you than anything she does.

- **Think Positively**

  Your relationship with his mother will probably go very well. She will most likely be loving, sane and authentic in her desire for her son's happiness. It is only a small minority of couples who encounter impregnable resistance to their love for each other, but we felt it necessary to prepare you for every possibility.

The statistical odds, based on our research, suggest that you will get the love and support of everyone in his family, including his mother. She will probably be crazy about you—eventually.

In keeping with our desire to thoroughly prepare you for every eventuality, we offer you the following tip sheet to help you understand and appropriately respond to whatever might come up during "The Talk." As always, we wish you the best.

Things his mother might say:	What she really means:	Your possible response:
"I just want him to have a normal life."	This is sick. It's not normal. I don't approve.	"This is normal for us."
"It can't possibly work."	I've never seen this and I don't understand it. It's too strange for me to comprehend.	"This is what we both want. We are happy. It *does* work for us."
"You've ruined the family"	I don't accept you. I don't like this and I will influence the entire family against you.	"I don't understand your statement. I thought you wanted your son's happiness." - or - "We feel our relationship can only *add* to the family." - or - "He loves his family *and* he loves me. We don't see a conflict here."
"I want him to be happy."	He can't possibly be happy with you—you're too old.	"He is happy. We are both very happy together." - or - "I'm glad you feel that way, because he is happy."
"Usually older women want to control and manipulate – he's young. He's impressionable. He's at risk here."	I assume you only want him because he is young and impressionable—and you can control him. That would be my only possible reason if I were in your shoes.	"You know your son is bright." (She doesn't dare argue that one). "He has good judgment—I would think you would trust the wise counsel you instilled in him." - or - "I'm sorry to hear that you don't trust him. I had no idea you thought he was so weak and directionless."

Things his mother might say:	What she really means:	Your possible response:
"He's far too young to be involved with you."	He should be involved with women his own age or younger.	"I find your son to be very mature. He obviously relates to me in a different way than he does to you. If he's going to be involved with anyone, wouldn't you rather it be a woman who really does love him and has his best interests at heart?"
"I won't stand for this."	I'll fight you tooth and nail. This is not what *I* want for my son.	"I'm sorry you feel that way. Your son and I are already together."
"Don't you think you're a little old to be doing these kind of things?"	I'll hit you hard on the age issue. I want to make you feel guilt and shame.	"Love doesn't see age anymore than it does race or religion. It sounds like you are returning to age discrimination." - or - "Obviously not." - or - "Age is only a number. Love is what counts."

Use good judgment and be brief in your responses. You don't need to defend yourself—you've done nothing wrong. Lengthy justifications and explanations aren't necessary. They only weaken your position.

His mother has her own process to go through as she works on adapting to a new and, for her, difficult situation. Your younger man wants you both in his life. You and he must be very patient and optimistic about your acceptance by his mother and the rest of his family. In many cases, you and your younger man's happiness together will eventually be accepted, but do not allow this to interfere with the growth and health of your relationship. After all, the life you are fashioning together belongs to the two of you first. Hopefully, you can also share your happiness with his family and yours.

Chapter 20

Help! His Mother is a Pit Bull

I realized that my mother didn't care about me or my happiness.
She was willing to put me on the rack in order to feel
safe and in control. When I saw that, I broke off all relations.
Dan (age 23)

Perhaps you've been as patient as long as you can and waited for the relationship between his mother and you to mature—to no avail. Yes, it can happen, especially if the younger man in question is very young (early twenties), still living at home—or has only very recently moved out on his own—and if his mother is controlling or manipulative or unable or unwilling to relinquish her position as the number one female in her son's life. While a mother's genuine concern for her son's happiness is certainly understandable, some family systems are so dysfunctional that it is not the son's happiness, but the mother's need for control that dominates the scenario. When that is the case, watch out, for the situation won't change. From what we've observed, it will only get worse. This type of mother's resistance to your relationship with her son will be as tenacious as a pit bull's bite. It will taint his entire family's perception of you and it will probably never be resolved.

Even in the healthiest of families, where love is secure and personal identity and freedom are encouraged, the young man's mother has valid reasons to be initially concerned and hesitant about a relationship between her son and a considerably older woman. For many of the couples we interviewed, the young man's mother simply didn't understand why a woman—often a woman close to her own age—would want to be with her son. Not because of any fault of his, but, because of the age difference, the mother couldn't see the basis of this unusual attraction.

I don't know what in the world she sees in him.
Marina (age 58)

Family approval was held in check while a "let's wait and see what happens" attitude prevailed. This is not inappropriate under the circumstances.

Motherhood is a job which demands an amazing degree of selflessness. For many women, it demands the sacrifice of their personal goals and desires in order to raise their children. Later, they're asked to let go of those children and reclaim the self they had put on hold or even completely abandoned. This is not an easy task for any woman, but some find it utterly impossible to separate their own identities from that of their children. It's been said that to some extent every family has some level of dysfunction. Certainly, every family has different issues with which the members must cope. As daughters, many of us have examined our own relationships with our mothers to determine what issues have shaped—or perhaps disfigured—our lives. Where sons are concerned, different configurations and permutations in the family dynamic can exist. In all of the cases we've seen where extreme hostility and resistance to the older woman/younger man relationship comes from his family, it ALWAYS originates with his mother. In fact, we only came across one instance where negativity was expressed by the father, but even there the resistance had to do with the fact that the older woman's divorce wasn't finalized and not because of the age difference.

Mother-in-law-from-hell jokes have long been a comedic staple among entertainers, but for some of the older women in our survey—and their younger men—it was no laughing matter. The mother who can't or won't relinquish her control over her son's choices will wreak havoc in his life (and yours, if you're involved with him) for years to come. If the couple meets and gets together by the time he's into his late twenties or older, he's had a chance to separate himself from her influence, at least to some degree. If he's in his early twenties, her influence is greater and his resistance to it is weaker.

The more threatened she is the more vigorous and tenacious will be her hostility towards you and her potential to destroy the relationship will be strong. If her attitude is that "it is her or me," she will view her very survival as a matriarchal figure to her son to be at stake and she will very likely force her son to sacrifice his own happiness for hers. This type of pressure on a young man is tremendous—family loyalty vs. his loyalty to you and himself. Talk about a no-win situation. This is a scenario dominated by pain and emotional abuse mysteriously identified by some of these mothers as love.

Twenty-three-year-old Dan told us about his mother's constant attacks on his girlfriend and the effect this had on his life:

> *She really put it to me. At first, I thought she cared and was just doing the protective mother thing. Then she let loose all barrels. She got the whole family involved. They all hated Melissa, because my mother did. They hadn't even met her. I got calls from everyone. Melissa wasn't invited to family get-togethers. She was totally cut out. My mother didn't even try to get to know her. They spoke a few times—but that was it. Melissa was an emotional wreck. I was upset.*
>
> *I really wanted to stay close to my family, but it was impossible. It never stopped—the lies, the manipulation, the emotional guilt—and I got tons of shame for "destroying our family."*
>
> *At one point, I hated Melissa. My mother really got into my head. I mean, I'd listened to her way for nineteen years and I trusted her. After a while, though, I realized that my mother didn't care about me or my feelings. She knew exactly what she was doing to me. She didn't care. I got into therapy—and then I really saw the game. Melissa was incredible during all this. She never pulled me the other way, away from my family.*
>
> *Melissa just wanted peace. I thought it was all about Melissa until my therapist showed me it was about me. My mother didn't really care about me or my happiness. She was willing to put me on the rack in order to feel safe and in control. When I saw that, I broke off all relations. My mother and the rest of the family didn't respect me or my choices. So I chose not to be with them.*

Particularly when the older woman is close to the mother's age, the threat of perceived competition rears its head. When Mom seeks to maintain control of her position as the primary female influence in her son's life, the battle begins.

> *There was no competition in my mind—his mother and I both had a place in his life. They were different places and each one was appropriate for who we were to him. Yet she always made me feel like "the other woman." It was like she was in love with him the way I was.*

Natalie (age 38)

Some mothers will stop at nothing to emerge victorious, as witnessed by Mark and Lisa, who had a seventeen-year age difference. Mark's mother went so far as to discredit Lisa in her new community with stories of her being sexually voracious, a woman who pulled young boys off the street. Twenty-six-year-old Mark's mom even used her considerable social network to try to get Lisa, forty-three, fired from her job. There was nothing she wouldn't do to get her son back. Lisa became the target for all of the mother's hatred and vengeance. The tools in her arsenal included character defamation, malicious lies and powerful community influence. As Lisa explained, Mark's mother's efforts were painfully felt:

> It was like I stepped into the Twilight Zone. Within six months, it seemed like everyone in town hated me, but no one knew me. She made sure she filled everyone's heads with lies in order to get me to leave town and get out of Mark's life for good.

The young men we interviewed shared a common theme. They were shocked, hurt and severely wounded by the poisonous love their mothers now revealed. This twisted, hurtful form of love robbed them of their mental and emotional well-being. As Mark related to us, his mother's actions took a devastating toll:

> I was torn. I loved my mother and I believed she loved me. She kept telling me things she had heard about Lisa—they were all lies, but after a while I didn't know who to believe. I'd known my mother my whole life— why would she lie to me? It caused fight after fight between Lisa and me. I couldn't take it. We'd break up, then get back together again, over and over. I finally had to believe what I felt inside about Lisa, but that meant seeing my mother for who she really was. It was the worst experience of my whole life.
>
> After five years, Lisa and I finally decided to separate. I can't think straight. I need to work out all this stuff with my family before I can see Lisa again. I know I love her, but I have to clear all this stuff with my mother and her dramas. I want to be with Lisa in the future, but I'm afraid that someone else will come into her life who doesn't have all these problems and I'll lose her forever.

Lisa tearfully described how she felt when she and Mark were finally driven apart:

> I had to move on. It was insanity. Beyond insanity. I've never met such a hate-filled family as Mark's. They made sure it was unbearable for us both. The damage that's been done to both of us is just too much. No one should have to go through this just to love another person. I wish we could work it out, but Mark is absolutely paralyzed now. He can't even work, he's so messed up. It's so senseless; it never had to be this way. But I'm just not staying in all this chaos and confusion.

When an overly controlling mother decides not to accept, like or value her son's choice of an older woman, her position usually doesn't change. Like a pit bull, her jaws are locked. Although a fairly small percentage (under 10 percent) of the couples we interviewed experienced this type of interference, ALL confirmed that the problem has continued to persist. Even when the couple stayed together through his thirties and even forties, his mother continued her campaign of harassment. The combination of a pit bull mother—often threatened, jealous, unempowered and desperate—and a union formed when the younger man is still *very* young, seems to be a recipe for lifelong difficulties and pain, if not outright failure of the relationship to survive. The mother who seeks to wound and even destroy her son to satisfy her own need for control will engage in relentlessly cruel and destructive behavior. This is often an unexpected, even shocking, reality for the couple to confront.

> *I thought she was concerned at first about him being hurt by our relationship. She was more upset when she discovered that we really loved each other. That just didn't make sense to me—she'd rather see him sleep with someone who didn't care for him, but hated me because I loved him.*
>
> **Connie (age 41)**

> *At first I assumed when she'd get to know me it would be all right and she would accept me. She was even polite in the beginning. But countless phone calls (to him) later, histrionic fits and intercession by every other family member just tore us apart. He couldn't handle it.*
>
> **Amy (age 39)**

> *She made his life so miserable that he developed bleeding ulcers. He could not take it and I could not take watching her tear his guts out. How is this love?*
>
> **Karen (age 42)**

> *I can't tell you the harm she did to both of us. It was incessant. She never gave up. It's been six years and she still is after me in every way possible. We can't even visit them—not because we wouldn't like to, it's just too uncomfortable. So now it looks like I really did take him away from her.*
>
> **Gayle (age 36)**

It takes tremendous courage on the part of both partners to withstand this kind of chronic interference. Because the man is younger, he is much more susceptible to his mother's demands. Both partners must see it for what it is and agree upon a course of action that works for them—and stick to it! Usually, if they are able to work through it and stay together, the younger man will be forced, against his will, to break off relations with his mother (and possibly the rest of his family) forever or for a period of time until they are able to honor and respect his choices.

Recognizing a Pit Bull Mother

- **Her Facade**

  She appears to control her family, usually through emotional blackmail and guilt, but she is actually insecure. She feels empty and worthless inside. Exerting control over others gives her a sense of inner stability and power. She does this either consciously or unconsciously, because she has no real power nor does she know how to develop any. She projects the façade of great power, usually from the role of victim.

- **Her Life**

  In the majority of cases, this woman has little or no interest in anything other than her family—and she expects them to provide what few rewards she is able to garner. We'll bet the ranch that you have a much bigger life than she does, so she's envious. She hates you because you've developed yourself in ways that she hasn't.

- **Her True Sweetheart**

  Her son is her connection. Her husband isn't really there, even if he is physically present. Her son is her life—her only source of feeling needed—and the appropriate boundaries of the mother/son relationship are blurred, projecting her son into the husband's role.

  She is a control freak and, whether she lives in an efficiency apartment or a well-appointed manor, the signs will be there. Pay attention to:

- **Her Energy**

  It is cold, uncomfortable and stiff. It's not you—that's just the way she is and that energy permeates her home. Even if her house was designed to impart a warm, homey atmosphere, it doesn't. You can feel the emptiness, the falseness. You may be fooled into thinking it's because she doesn't like or feel comfortable with you. Don't be misled. This is her home which contains her energy. It will feel just as cold after you leave.

- **Her Decor**

  Forget Feng Shui, flow or freedom. Even the attempt to cozy it up will not make her environment warm and comfortable. There will be hard edges, a rigid structure, making you feel restricted and trapped everywhere you move.

- **Her Furnishings**

  Mostly uncomfortable and non functional. Remember, you are not supposed to stay!

■ **Her Animals**
If any, they are strange. You might be advised *not* to pet the cat (it may scratch) or the dog (it may bite). She may even tell you that the animal "doesn't like strangers." Do you really think she's describing the animal?

■ **Her Personal Effects**
Note the framed photograph of her son. It's the largest, most prominent one of him alone. It is meant to commemorate the last time he was totally controllable. Is he five? Seventeen? She may tell you, "We're a very close family." In that case, you'll find additional framed photos—usually of other relatives congregated in a large pack and all looking miserable. You will notice the absence of pictures of her husband or his family—he is, after all, nonexistent. Remember, everything has its proper place with her, including her son.

■ **Her Husband**
He's not there. Expect to hear upon your arrival that "he's working" or "he's away" or "he's sleeping." Even if he is there, he's absent. He's watching television, reading a book or involved in some solitary task. He's an escape artist. He has little emotional investment left in her or his family. He doesn't care about you and hardly knows his son.

Pit Bull Progeny

Of course, pit bull mothers come attached to men of all ages, as most experienced women have already discovered along the way. Is there anything worse than a pit bull mother? Yes, if the pit bull mother has succeeded in raising a pit pup son, commonly referred to as a "mama's boy." He will cling as tenaciously to her as she does to him. In that case, he will never leave mama to make you (or any woman) his priority.

An older "mama's boy" is, however, easier to identify than a younger one. If he's forty-five years old, has had numerous failed relationships and is in daily telephone contact with his mom (or even lives with her), those are strong clues. But when the man in question is still very young, you often just don't know what you're getting into. Even if he wants desperately to be with you, he's still significantly influenced by his mother. So keep your eyes open, heed the signals and proceed with great caution.

Chapter 21

Handling Her Family

Some of her family talked to me like a runny-nosed,
crayon-eating, bed-wetting kid and others welcomed me
with open arms. I received both ends of the spectrum.
Jared (age 26)

Exploring attitudes about and obstacles to the older woman/younger man relationship from the viewpoint of the older woman's family, we found that far fewer problems existed. Perhaps because she is older and has had more opportunity to reflect upon what she wants, her family has had time to make their own attitudinal adjustments. Because she's no longer young, they may have given up trying to change or control her. When fears were expressed, they mirrored the existing stereotypes we've already identified: He'll leave her for a younger woman; he's only using her (for sex or money or connections); he's less emotionally invested than she is; he won't be able to make a commitment. Ironically, we found that when the older woman/younger man relationships did break up, over 80 percent of the time the women initiated it. Mutually agreed upon breakups constituted 15 percent of the relationships we studied. It was only in 5 percent of the cases that the younger men left the older women. Most of the time, she left him. These figures do give us cause to rethink some of the commonly held beliefs and misconceptions about these relationships. And, by the way, of the 5 percent of the younger men who did leave their relationships, it *wasn't* for other (or younger) women. They just bailed. Fears, pressures and complications beyond their level of maturity were the reasons cited, with only one case that of a man who wanted to start a family, but couldn't with his older partner.

Regarding the often expressed fear, "He'll hurt you," we wonder how many people today seriously expect any guarantees from love relationships. We also wonder why young women who marry same age or older partners aren't counseled by their families, "Be careful. You might get hurt. When he turns forty-five, he might leave you for his secretary, or—worse yet—your best friend. He might decide to dump you and leave you penniless while he gets hair plugs, a sports car and a trophy wife." It's odd, we think, that young women aren't warned about those possibilities (and older women are) even though, statistically, it is the young women who are more likely to suffer such fates.

Her Mother

We found that most mothers of daughters involved with younger men were concerned about their daughters' emotional well-being, citing a customary and predictable litany of concerns. Many were also perplexed and couldn't understand why their daughters would be interested in younger men. In their day, an older man was frequently considered quite a catch—worldly, sophisticated and very desirable socially. Although they didn't understand their daughters' choice, they often still tried to be supportive while expressing their concerns.

Generally, the mothers of older women involved in happy relationships with younger men, while initially hesitant, came around eventually. Only one mother in our survey never quite got over her discomfort.

> My sister approved, but my mother didn't handle it very well. Although she stayed with us for several weeks in the beginning, I learned from my sister that she did not "approve of my lifestyle." Here I was, forty-three years old and he was still in his early twenties. My assumption is that it wasn't because we were living together (unmarried), but really because of the age difference.
>
> **Penny (age 62)**

More indicative of the norm are the following responses:

> My mother and grandmothers were positive. Everyone else expressed concern for me, stating, "We just don't want to see you get hurt." When it ended, they said, "Just as well. Now find someone your own age."
>
> **Ellen (age 39)**

> My mother was concerned. She'd never heard of anything like this before. She thought I was a little nuts, I guess. She kept telling me, "It can't work, you know." Then she met Fred. She still thought he was too young for me, but she really liked him. He's so sweet, so open and real. At least it

dispelled the thought in her mind that he would hurt me. Mother and Fred
became close, as I did with his family. Finally, everyone saw that we were
really happy and that, even though they didn't understand how, our rela-
tionship worked.

Tina (age 47)

When I first told my mother about Bryan, I expected her to totally
freak out. Her image of my perfect man was a powerful industrialist who
could install me in an estate in Connecticut. Bryan certainly wasn't that. I
mean, he was an auto mechanic and twenty-three. When I told her, there was
a long silence. Then she asked me, "Is this serious?" When I said yes, she said,
"As your mother, you know it's not my choice for you. But if it makes you
happy, really happy, then do it."

Elizabeth (age 41)

I didn't know how my mother would take it, but I had been alone for a
long time and she really wanted me to have a loving man by my side. When
she met Craig she was a little surprised, but she was happy for both of us.

Coleen (age 40)

Children and Other Family Members

Reactions from the rest of the family can be mixed. We were particularly surprised that in our survey we came across no overly suspicious and protective sons. As far as the women's children were concerned, some loved their
new dad—or mom's new boyfriend—and some responded negatively as
many children do to the upheavals created by new stepparents or the blend-
ing of two families. A new man on the scene can be unsettling for youngsters whatever the circumstances, but it is the quality of the man and his
relationship with the woman's children that will usually determine the ultimate outcome.

He is a wonderful father to my children—a fact they appreciate even
more now that they are older. My daughters have chosen him to give them
away at their weddings, despite their having a good relationship with their
father. I think that says a lot. He is loving and supportive and he's my soul
mate. I don't think many people find theirs.

Pat (age 51)

My mother, sister and brother felt that I was entitled to a relationship
that brought happiness. Two of my children resented him, but felt as though
I had given so much of myself to raising them that they respected my choice.
The other two also resented him and my relationship with them has been
strained since that time. They felt as though I should have married someone

that I had a ten-year relationship with and, by not marrying him and living with him instead, I ruined their lives.

Alana (age 58)

When I brought Bill home, he and my son started playing video games. They were close in age. They really clicked with each other. Later, my son said, "Good for you, Mom. He's cool." I think he had seen how much pain I'd gone through with his father and how hard the divorce was on me. He was just happy to see me happy again.

Mary Anne (age 40)

It was my son who introduced Oliver to me. It took three years for us to become a romantic couple. When I finally did tell my son about our relationship, he was very calm. He wasn't shocked, even though Oliver and he are close to the same age. I think he saw it coming. He was, I think, relieved. He felt that I had found something that was really giving me happiness. Now, twenty-five years later and after ten years of marriage, my whole family adores him, including my eldest son. Believe it or not, my children relate to him as a parent, even though my youngest son is only five years younger than Oliver.

Penny (age 62)

We found that the majority of the older women's daughters expressed great joy in seeing their mothers happy again. We heard many stories of difficult divorces, dead-end dates and lonely nights. They were relieved to see their mothers discover love again, along with a renewed sense of hope.

I can see why my mom would attract a younger guy. She's a fun person. It makes a lot of sense to me. When she was getting serious with Kevin, my first reaction was, "Oh well, you need someone younger to keep up with you." Kevin is a great guy. Everyone in our family just loves him. He was making her happy and she was so unhappy after the divorce.

Maggie (age 30)

While most of the older women's children were receptive, there can be cases where children are resentful and confused. They may decide to make the younger men targets for their own anger.

Danny hated me being with Walter. He didn't know him and didn't want to. My son was already having trouble in school—the divorce was especially hard on him—so this just added to his problems. He put up a wall—and it hasn't come down.

Trish (age 37)

Where children are concerned, either his or yours, if adverse reactions continue unabated, we suggest family counseling. While any new partner in the family can be upsetting to a child, the older woman/younger man relationship can be particularly confusing. It may seem especially strange to your children if he is close to their age or to his children if you are closer to their grandmother's age. This is an uncommon situation and they have no point of reference. Accepting differences may be quite uncomfortable for them, especially if they are adolescents and very invested in conformity. Patience, love and understanding are key. Give them time to make the emotional adjustment. Allow them to express their feelings without censure. Good parenting is not age related. Many of our respondents encountered a period of problematic behavior from children who later not only bonded with the new partners, but experienced a deep affection and closeness with them.

Dealing with family members can be tricky business. We can certainly "fire a friend" and cut off outside acquaintances who don't support us, but our family is inherited and not so easily dismissed. While reactions may cover a broad spectrum, we have found that most family members do come around in time.

At the beginning, they felt that he might have been using me, but then again, how? He was in a far better financial state than I was at that particular time. Through his great business sense, I made some investments with him from which I still derive benefit.

Claire (age 62)

They were just surprised that she was dating me first of all. It was interracial so that was different for them. They had a tough time accepting that at first, even more than the age gap. After they got to know me, they were okay with it.

Michael (age 27)

My mother and sister were a bit cautious. My sister, who is ten years younger than I, made many comments about my robbing the cradle and asked me what I could possibly have in common with someone that age. Mom was a bit more concerned about my well-being since I'd recently ended an eight-year relationship with a man who emotionally abused me. Dad was understanding since he'd left my mother after twenty-nine years for a woman sixteen years younger than he. Ethan's siblings are all close to my age. Ethan was their baby brother. I am, in fact, older than all of them. The oldest of his siblings chides me still about being the "old woman" in the family. Mostly, they have been loving and supportive. Ethan's mom knew me beforehand in a professional capacity. I sensed she was a bit protective of

her baby initially—but we are now the best of friends. Ethan's dad and step-
mom were always accepting of me. However, since his father isn't that much
older than I am, I think he cringes a bit when I call him Dad.

Phyllis (age 47)

If you are experiencing problems with your younger man, are torn or
have doubts, share these only with the most trusted and supportive friends
and/or therapists. Any discomfort you express about your relationship will
provide ambivalent or disapproving family members with an opportunity
in their conversations with you to reflect back to you your own insecurities.
They will ultimately treat the relationship with the same level of comfort
and confidence you project. Hearing your fears will catalyze their own.
Family members, more than others, feel free to share negative emotions.
Protect yourself by adopting a positive attitude and letting everyone share
in only the good things in the relationship.

We hope your family embraces your choice, but if some members don't,
please remember it is *your* choice that counts. You deserve to be with the
man who makes you happy. Don't let their fears or disapproval taint your
affection for your younger man. As we have seen, in time most of the emotional dust settles and the younger men are integrated into the family. At
the beginning, it's a new experience for everyone and it takes time to be
accepted and understood by all concerned. If your family members really
do love you, ultimately they will want what is best for you. So live your life
and take heart.

Chapter 22

Their Stories

He has been incredibly attentive and very loving towards me.
He spoils me. When I least expect it, Miguel surprises me
with some thoughtful gesture of kindness.
Rita (age 45)

When the age difference between an older woman and a younger man is great, more than the usual number of questions arise. How did they meet? Who initiated it? How long did it last? We decided to let some of these couples tell you their stories in their own words. Colleen, fifty-one, and Ned, forty-one, have been together for almost a quarter of a century:

I was twenty-nine, returning to college to finish my bachelor's degree. I had three kids—six years to two months—and had been a house mom since my first was born. I was married to a spoiled (by me) workaholic who had no interest in me beyond sex and supper. We had been on the edge of separation for two years when I returned to school. Ned was "the cute kid in the second row." There were only five to six men in a class of 100 and a group of us used to gather for coffee, to study or have a couple of beers after exams. Ned was always part of this group and he interested me more and more.

One night after I'd known him about three months, we were all in the pub. One girl (his age) was obviously making a play for him. I decided it was time to see if he was interested in me at all or if I was really off base and making a fool of myself. I turned all my attention to him and he dumped her immediately. As I was still married and he lived at home, our time together was only at school. We were wildly attracted to each other sexually and a few

months later we were sleeping together. Two months after that my husband
moved out and Ned basically moved in. It was a very stormy time, lots of highs
and lows. I couldn't see myself divorced, but couldn't imagine my life without
Ned. Twenty-three years down the road we are still very happy together. We
have our share of arguments as we're both stubborn, but we both realize that
our relationship is very important and we work to keep connected.

One of our favorite stories of a satisfying relationship was told to us by an
eighty-year-old woman named Karolina whom we have mentioned before.
We spent a day talking to her about her twenty-five-year relationship with
Paolo, a man sixteen years her junior. She told us about her life growing up
in Sweden and marrying her first husband who was only a few years older
than she. Their relationship had been marked by his excessive drinking and
constant quest of young women. This was, of course, a great heartache for
her. Karolina worked and when she became the "breadwinner" in the family
fourteen years later, she finally had the opportunity to divorce him. Concern
for her daughter's well-being occupied her for several years, but after that she
was free to love again.

This time, the gentleman was several years older than she was and quite
successful. He had retired and they moved to a very chic and exclusive island
in the Mediterranean. After a relatively short time together, he became ter-
minally ill and she nursed and took care of him for the next four years until
he died. Such was her love life up to that time.

At fifty-five she was still beautiful, vibrant, wealthy and alone again. Two
men fought for her attention. One was elderly, sophisticated and socially
prominent and the other, a thirty-nine year-old. While she was urged by her
family and friends to take the sure bet—the older man—her response was to
say, "I don't want to play nursemaid to another man."

Initially, when Paolo (the thirty-nine-year-old man) began paying attention
to her, she thought it was only out of kindness. He offered to drive her to do
her errands (she did not drive.) He helped her with household repairs. He
made himself available to her as a friend or so she thought. It never occurred
to Karolina that Paolo looked upon her as a mate. He was so young. Surely,
he was only feeling sorry for her. But when the truth of his intentions
dawned on her, she chose Paolo, much to the dismay of her now fifty-year-
old daughter, Brit:

I wanted my mother to be with the older man. He was perfect. Elegant,
sophisticated and wealthy. I really pushed her, but she wouldn't hear of it.
One year later, the man gave up and married another woman. Six months
later he had a massive stroke and was confined to a wheelchair for the rest
of his life. My mother was right. She would have been a nursemaid again
had she chosen him.

Still not accepting their union, however, Brit echoed the censure Karolina and Paolo experienced on the island. The age difference was radical and quite extreme for that time period, even in Europe. The couple chose to leave the island and move to Portugal, where they have lived together happily for the past twenty-five years. Brit continued:

> At first I was extremely embarrassed by it. I didn't want to introduce them to my friends in the States, because Paolo looked so young. And I really could not understand why he would want an older woman. I thought he was after her money, even though he had sufficient money of his own. Now, twenty-five years later, the way it looks to me is "Good for her!" I have accepted it. I am proud of it now, because he loves and adores her. He treats her like gold. I enjoy seeing her happy and Paolo is such a wonderful person. But I was twenty-five at the time they became a couple and the world was different. It took me about, oh, ten years to accept it. Now, I'm so happy for them both.

How ironic, we thought, that husband number one chased young women relentlessly, while his former wife ended up with an adoring man sixteen years her junior. Both Paolo and Karolina told us, however, that the pain of the social pressure had been enormous.

Considering the time period and strict social codes to which they had been exposed, their union has been difficult to say the least. Both Karolina and Paolo expressed their heartfelt concern for others who might be experiencing this kind of painful judgment and outside pressure. Though their road has been a hard one, their love and common goals have kept them together despite the odds against them. We promised this delightful couple that we would share their story as tangible evidence of the power of love—which knows no age.

Another story that moved us because it defied all the odds was that of Penny (age sixty-two) and Oliver (age forty-six) who have also been together for twenty-five years and married for the past ten years. Penny described how their relationship began:

> Oliver was nineteen and I was thirty-five. My son brought him home. I was teaching music at the time and my son said, "Have I got a student for you." I was teaching classical guitar. I started teaching him and we were simpatico from day one. I was aware that this young man had something very unique. He had the talent and the intelligence...it happened through the music. That was how we initially began the communication.
>
> He was a rock guitarist and I was teaching him classical guitar. I ultimately got him into the college where I was teaching music. He was very gifted and bright and we became rather close friends. I was going though a

divorce. My estranged husband was very abusive and a master manipulator. Oliver and I would talk. He was a great listener.

At one point, it was like a marathon. Oliver and I were up for three days, no sleep, no nothing, trying to strategize my way through this ugly divorce, trying to understand what was happening in my life. It was so strange, but I needed someone to speak to and he was so comforting. But still, we didn't begin a physical relationship, we were just extremely close. The romantic attraction started about then, but we didn't play it out. I was afraid to...at least until the divorce became finalized.

The minute it did become final, we culminated the relationship. I didn't tell anyone...we had known each other over three years before we became involved. Then I moved to Arizona with my son and Oliver went into the Army. These were financial moves for Oliver and me—we both needed money. When he came to visit me, the relationship really accelerated. We both knew we wanted to be together. Even knowing that, we were on and off for the next few years because he felt he wanted children. That was an issue for us. He told me he'd live with me, but couldn't marry me for that reason. I made the decision that I wasn't going through pregnancy and motherhood again. This was our only real problem—on the inside. He had to come to terms with not being able to have a family. So we didn't have contact for awhile. I had to stick to my decision. I had to be able to live my own life. He agreed, very reluctantly, to not contact me at all. I went on with my work. One day I walked into my office and was told he had called. It was under the pretense of being a "family matter" and we agreed to meet the following night. We ended up spending the weekend together and that was it. We decided we were not going to live apart. We have been together ever since and eventually we married. It's been ten years now since our marriage.

As Phyllis explained, she and Ethan (seventeen years difference) exhibited a mutually adventurous spirit from the start of their nine-year relationship:

Ethan and I met in a yoga class. I was with my boyfriend. Ethan was the guy who fell asleep and snored during class. Later, we met again on a beach. I came onto the beach with my boyfriend and two friends, one of whom had MS. The woman was in a wheelchair and we needed to shield her from the wind. There was a big boulder (we still refer to it as our rock) and it was directly in front of Ethan and his friend's blanket. I walked up to them and asked if it would be all right to plant ourselves right in front of them. They graciously said it was fine. Ethan claims that throughout the time we were there he was ogling me and wondering if I was checking him out. I wasn't, but he imagined I had. You see, Ethan had just that day returned from a kayaking trip across the Sound to one of the islands off Martha's Vineyard. Out in the middle of the ocean, he had had a strong sense of a woman. In any case, there were several more meetings over a period of a year when Ethan made it known to me that he was enamored. I was still with my boyfriend and, although flattered, simply had no interest. I was housecleaning on the Vineyard and Ethan happened to come to visit the house where I was working. He was on his way to Costa Rica and as he was leaving he walked up and gave me a very passionate kiss on the lips. I was bowled over. Suddenly, this young man became more than a flirtation. I was interested. My boyfriend and I were having problems—we had many of them over our eight years together. During the month that Ethan was in Costa Rica, my boyfriend and I broke up. I was quite distraught. Ethan sent me a postcard and that cinched it. I remember it was an April afternoon off Lucy Vincent Beach and I just had this powerful sense of Ethan and a willingness to give it a try. Once he came back, I sent him a card that said in not so many words that I was available. He called and we set up a date for a walk on the beach. We saw each other every day after that and I realized that this was no ordinary twenty-one-year-old. We both had issues of co-dependency from past relationships and decided to try not seeing each other for three out of the seven days in the week so we could both maintain our separate identities. This was very beneficial in the long run, although we weakened after a month or so and began seeing each other every day again. He moved in after we were together for six months. We lived together until we were married two years later.

Sometimes, even a fairly brief affair lends itself to a memorable story, as did that of Ellen, age thirty-nine, and Joe, age twenty-five. Ellen told us of their romance:

Joe and I met in a Spanish class. When he walked into the room, there was an instant attraction. The desks were set up in a square arrangement and he sat across from me. I knew after the first night of class that he would sit next to me and he did for the next four months. After our final exam, I knew he would wait for me so that just the two of us could go for a drink and celebrate. And, of course, he did. I then went away for a long weekend and mailed him a postcard with the message in Spanish. I knew he would call when he received it and he did.

We had an incredible summer. I had never been so happy. We had romantic picnics in Central Park listening to the Philharmonic, ferry rides as the sun set or we held hands and walked or rollerbladed along the promenade of Battery Park. He wrote me love poems, would surprise me with tickets to Shakespeare in the Park and would meet me for a lunchtime kiss.

This all ended shortly after Labor Day when the financial package he anticipated getting from the university fell far short of what he would need. With his tail between his legs, he returned to New Hampshire disappointed in himself and depressed.

We tried to stay together for a little over a year long distance, but the intimacy created over the summer could not be recreated with me in New

York and him in New Hampshire. Relationships are built around daily activities. A good example is when friends that you do everything with either move or get married. While you are still "friends," it is never the same no matter how hard you try. That is what happened with Joe and me. So now, six months after our relationship ended, we talk on the phone every week or so, usually for about an hour. For now, I'm glad we can remain friends. Fortunately, friendship was the basis of our relationship.

One story, in particular, helped us remember to keep things in perspective. Josepha, age fifty-four, reminded us of what really counts, as she talked about her life with Kevin, age forty-one:

We actually met when I was hired to work in his office. At one point, when I knew he was going through a difficult time, I invited him over to my condo, along with a couple of friends. We had a good time that night and started to see each other outside of the office more and more often.

A couple of months later we went away on vacation to Puerto Rico together (my mother's homeland, which I had never seen) and became fully romantically involved. Later in that year, I was no longer able to work due to an automobile accident.

We have been through many very difficult times together over the last seven years. But the one thing that stands out is that we respect each other and have learned to communicate better with each other. Communication has become the key to addressing any issue. We share a deep love for each other. Not that we don't have major challenges in front of us, but we are both positive influences in each other's lives.

As I said before, I don't think that age is such a big factor in a relationship. It is the two people involved. Where are they in their spiritual growth? Even though age is a factor, beyond that, does the couple have things in common to share? Are they connected on some level? Do they share common goals? What do they want to get out of life? Do they enhance each other's experience on this planet?

During the time that we were writing this book, our friend, Rita, met and became seriously involved with a man thirteen years her junior. We love this story because, of all our close friends, Rita seemed like the least likely candidate to enter into this kind of relationship.

By the age of forty-six, Rita was a very sophisticated woman. Divorced, with a grown son, she was a world traveler who had lived abroad on two continents and was accustomed to men of both means and power. Rita preferred older men, found them attractive and had frequently insisted to us that older men could be the most outrageously wonderful lovers. Although Rita had dated and been involved with a number of men, none of her relationships had ended happily. Rita, like so many women, had suffered deceitfulness, emotional unavailability and downright rudeness at the hands of these men. Her response had been to develop a hard crust around her heart. She'd been hurt and disappointed one time too many.

Although Miguel, age thirty-three, worked in the same office as Rita and they enjoyed a friendly, teasing kind of repartee, she never thought of him as having relationship potential. Although she found him very attractive, he was, in her mind, a sort of younger brother. Miguel was the office "computer nerd"—hardly one of the power brokers with whom she came into daily contact. As Rita explained:

Miguel was interested in me before I was aware of that fact. There was always a mutual attraction between us at work in terms of joking and teasing, but he did that with everyone so I didn't think he was especially interested in me. Other people in the office noticed it, but I didn't.

One day, Rita's home computer, which she relied on for her job, needed some kind of adjustment. Miguel came over to see what was needed. They talked. They talked some more and they continued to talk late into the night. They didn't have sex, but Rita woke up the next morning with Miguel's arms wrapped tightly around her. They have been seeing one another ever since.

Knowing Rita's penchant for older, wealthier, more worldly men, we were curious about what it was about Miguel that had beguiled her. Was it his youth? Was it that he had tight abdominal muscles and taut, firm skin? Not exactly. What captured Rita was precisely what Miguel had in common with many of the men who have been raised in the era of feminist consciousness. He, Rita told us, was clearly more evolved:

He has been incredibly attentive and very loving towards me. He spoils me. When I least expect it, Miguel surprises me with some thoughtful gesture of kindness...like leaving long-stemmed roses on my bed or a present under my pillow. He has written me wonderfully romantic letters telling me how much I mean to him. None of my older boyfriends had ever done that.

Miguel will often surprise me by organizing dinner and he always insists upon doing the dishes if I prepare a meal. I take special note of this, because I've had the experience of being left with a kitchen full of dirty dishes late on a work night, while the man I was seeing went home without even an offer to help. Another time, a former boyfriend invited me to what I thought was to be an intimate dinner for two at his home. When I arrived, he pointed to the kitchen, said he had invited eight other people and wanted me to start cooking. I walked out in disgust.

Miguel once organized a weekend canoeing trip during a time I desperately needed to get out of the city. He really planned it out. On another occasion, I returned to my desk after lunch and found an envelope containing five

Yankee playoff tickets with a poetic letter comparing the thrills and disap-
pointments of baseball to the ups-and-downs of relationships. Not only did he
want to be the first to take me to a professional baseball game, but he also invit-
ed my girlfriend and her two children. I couldn't believe his thoughtfulness.

Miguel doesn't play games. He has shared so much of himself with me
and he expresses his feelings honestly. He also doesn't expect me to just give
up my own needs and desires to take care of his. With the older men I've
dated, I have often felt I wasn't being heard, that my feelings were being dis-
counted.

What was not very surprising to us, however, were the initial doubts in
both Rita and Miguel's minds:

I didn't really think about the age difference at first, but once I was
actually involved with him and began to understand the depths of his emo-
tional maturity, his basic values and outlook on life and learned of the many
similar turns our lives have taken (we both have former medical backgrounds
and worked in Africa), my feelings for him went off the Richter scale. At that
point, I did ask myself, "What does Miguel see in me? Why would he want
to date someone thirteen years older?" I found out later that he was hesitant,
too, because he felt that I could have any man I wanted and that man would
be more powerful and financially successful, so why would I want to date
him, just a computer guy.

Rita's story, like so many others, is that of a woman being made to feel
shame for making the same kind of choice for which a man is generally
applauded. How dare she make a choice which exclaims to the world that she
is still a sexual being, not willing to be put out to pasture simply because she
is past a certain age? Is it any wonder that, although more and more older
women and younger men are finding love and satisfaction with each other, so
relatively few are willing to come forth?

If you are reading this and wondering how widespread these relationships
really are, we suggest the next time you find yourself at a dinner party or
some other social gathering bring up the subject of older women/younger
men relationships and ask who knows someone who has had one. We believe
you'll be surprised by how many of the other guests suddenly remember that
they had an uncle or a former business associate, neighbor, dentist, sibling of
a close friend, doctor, lawyer or even Indian Chief who was married to or living with an older woman or younger man. We'll wager their stories are as
wonderfully diverse and interesting as they are.

Chapter 23

Their Advice

Please do not let age be the thing that keeps you from experiencing a potentially wonderful relationship.
Kathryn Janus, psychotherapist

In gathering material on older women/younger men, we realized that we needed to interview couples, as well as individual women and men who had at one time been involved in this type of relationship. At first we talked to friends and acquaintances in the hope of uncovering some true-life stories and later we expanded our research to include interviews of the couples themselves. What we didn't expect was that everyone we talked to knew someone who not only had been involved in such a relationship, but wanted to talk to us about it. As we added additional men and women to our study, we realized this was a hot topic with more and more people overcoming their reticence and, in some cases, embarrassment and wanting to share their experiences, thoughts and feelings.

Above all, we wanted these individuals to give our readers advice on how to handle older women/younger men relationships. With their wide spectrum of experience, we asked them to enlighten us and share not only what worked, but also what didn't work.

Regarding the common problem many older women have of feeling they are being compared physically and emotionally to younger women, we discovered the most prevalent advice was: Be yourself. Self-acceptance is a primary requirement in giving yourself permission to be who you really are.

If I see a fifty-year-old woman who's trying to look twenty-five, I think she's ridiculous. Too much plastic surgery, too much wearing young girl's clothes and she becomes a joke. It's good to take care of yourself, go to the gym, eat well, etc. But too much trying to be something else is a turnoff. If you're that interested in changing yourself, something is wrong with you.

Josh (age 43)

We were also told:

I feel (and my partner does too) that our relationship is not only special, but unique. When we are together, we forget about the age difference. The only advice I could impart is not to compete with the younger women. If he wants you for who you are, face the competition, but don't join them. If he wants you to change your appearance, by all means do so, but only if you also want to. In my own situation, at the time we began our relationship, I looked far younger than I was. Today, naturally I appear older, but not quite as old as I am. But time is unforgiving and that's something we all have to deal with in our own way. There is no other generalization I could impart, because the older woman/younger man relationship is totally dependent on the individuals involved, their level of maturity, what they expect from their partners and whether or not they are seeking commitment.

Astrid (age 61)

The thing that women don't understand is that men are always going to be looking at other women—the most faithful man will look. Whether they take it beyond looking is a matter of personality, maturity and character.

If women could just trust themselves and who they are—be confident in that—there's nothing more compelling. I would say don't compare yourself to Pamela Anderson...and just realize the guy, the young guy, really wants you.

Nigel (age 37)

Keep an open mind and do not underestimate your partner because he is younger. Age is not always a requirement for maturity. Be what you are. Do not try to compete with a younger woman for your partner's attention. Keep your relationship alive by never demonstrating boredom, but instead find common interests and elaborate on them. Of course, it goes without saying that you must keep up your appearance, since this not only gives you the confidence you need in this type of relationship, but warrants a healthy respect from your partner as well.

Robert (age 40)

As in our earlier chapter, Communication In the Bedroom, the same advice is given here: "Don't compare; enjoy." So you're forty and he's twenty-six—should you be obsessively hunting the makeup aisles for anti-wrinkle creams, shopping for navel-baring tops in the teen department and rocking out to Gen-X music? No—not unless *you* want to. You don't have to be his age or look his age. If that's what he wanted, he wouldn't have chosen you.

Women need to know that the real way to maintain a youthful attitude and outlook is through continued growth and exploration. The concept of aging, whether accurate or not, implies fixed ideas, limited interests and strong preferences. Rather than contracting and narrowing your life, we believe the older woman/younger man relationship fosters personal expansion.

My advice to an older woman involved with a younger man is to quit worrying about the age difference and absorb some of his energies. Let him teach you all the things you were afraid to do on your own—scuba diving, riding a Harley, snowboarding. Younger men like to keep moving, experimenting, growing. Don't think because you're older and have "been there" that yours is the only way. He doesn't care about your stretch marks; he wants to make love to you all night long. He'll adore you forever if you'll let him. For my forty-fifth birthday, David rented a helicopter as a surprise. We flew at sunset out over the desert to a great hilltop overlooking the Colorado River. When the pilot set us down there, David unpacked roses, champagne and chilled crab cocktails to share as the full moon came up. Show me an older guy with that much romantic creativity. I am blessed.

Pat (age 51)

The key to success is: willingness to try new experiences; willingness to learn about your partner's interests; willingness to give (age can make us very narrow in our opinions and selfish with our time).

Denise (age 44)

What works is openness to his friends, family and interests, ignoring the negative people and learning from his perspective and experiences. What doesn't work is imposing my level of "experience" as the only yardstick.

Jill (age 47)

Along with the fear of not looking younger or being younger, many women also experience severe blocks around the entire age issue. Although it is, indeed, *their* issue, many choose to project their problem onto the younger men with whom they are involved. Older women second-guess these men's intentions, criticize their lack of maturity or resist involvement.

We met at a singles dance. I had put off having an intimate relationship and decided the time was right. While at the dance, I eyed the most spectacular woman I had ever seen and figured if she said no to a dance with me, I would leave. As fate would have it, she came and stood beside me. I offered to light her cigarette. I pursued her from that moment on. It was difficult because I felt I was focusing on who she was and she was only looking at our age disparity. This is a constant nuisance that I feel will always be around, but I think we are getting better at ignoring it. Our age is not who we are. When we started seeing one another, Pat would say, "Don't fall in love with me. You're too young for me." This is very damaging to the younger man who only wants to be with the woman and yet is constantly being rejected because of a number.

Doug (age 31)

What doesn't work? Making demeaning comments about a lack of knowledge because of his youth; having a know-it-all attitude; constant jealousy caused by younger women and a possessive attitude; taking your partner for granted and perhaps showing him off as a trophy to your friends; and never ever press for that "piece of paper" to hold him. In an older woman/younger man relationship, since man is the perennial hunter, let him keep wooing you. Don't chase him. He may hide.

Sarah (age 58)

I told him not to fall in love with me, because he was too young and I wasn't willing to get involved with a younger man because of my preconceived ideas. I thought it would make me feel old. It had the opposite effect and I have never felt so adored. I was self-conscious in public at first, but now I am not. We are a very attractive couple and are so in love, people only smile and envy us. I really love being with someone so handsome, devoted and virile. There is never a dull moment.

Nicole (age 36)

The people we interviewed felt very strongly about the perceived "age issue." Many had to jump over their own hurdles (both mentally and culturally) to be in these types of partnership. They reminded us what was truly important, and that is to take the focus off the age difference and redirect it toward the relationship.

Don't get too analytical. If you're open to it—and she's open to it, just do it. If you try to break it down, you can get lost in that tangle. It's a relationship and she's older, so?

Ahmad (age 40)

Don't let age get in the way! You are a person and know feelings when you have them. Trust them and nothing else. The challenge is to overcome what the world thinks and just enjoy yourself, because there is so much to enjoy. Inevitably, I feel the older person questions the loyalty of the younger person, because our society places so much emphasis on youth and not enough on wisdom. This will always be an obstacle that raises itself throughout the relationship. If this is overcome, however, the opportunities are boundless. It's great being able to be myself with someone I love.

As long as you keep age out of the relationship, you should only experience "normal" relationship problems that plague anyone at any age. Age is just a number.

Mark (age 35)

Age is just a number. The most important thing in an older woman/younger man relationship is mutual respect, friendship and trust. These are the same qualities that are important in all relationships.

Ellen (age 39)

Another area of wisdom that the women and men with whom we talked wanted to share had to do with what works in older woman/younger man relationships or what can be done to make them work. Communication, not surprisingly, came up a lot:

Communicate—better than you've ever communicated in your life. Every little thing that's bothering you has to be confronted. No matter how painful or awkward or guilt-inducing that subject may be—communicate. Talk, talk, talk. And if a lack of communication causes problems—get out. Because if you can't communicate now, it's only going to get worse as you both get older. If you can't communicate, then he or she is not right for you and you need to move on.

Lenny (age 38)

Age does not make such a difference in a relationship. What matters most are the people involved in the relationship. It works when the communication is open and free and it doesn't work when the communication is limited. Communication is the key. I can't stress that enough.

Marie (age 52)

Keep an open attitude and communicate. As to your behavior, be yourself...and if you are as lucky as I am, you will experience one of the highest levels of honesty possible between two people.

Fred (age 28)

Challenges revolve more around responding to and dealing with negative reactions from family and friends. I learned not to worry too much about the opinions of others as long as I truly believed I was right. The opportunities, on the other hand, are limitless. As in any relationship, communication is paramount.

Monica (age 40)

Other advice on making the relationship work:

Establish it as a serious, stable relationship, i.e. bring him to family events, have family/friends get to know him as a person and see him as a whole person and not just a guy who "will be around for a brief interlude."

Rebecca (age 46)

I think it's important to find somebody you're compatible with socially. Obviously there has to be a very strong attraction. That's probably the most important requirement, because you'll have many people doubting that it can work. The foundation of the relationship must be strong—so outside influences cannot come in and break it up. Most importantly, you have to be open to the possibilities in such a relationship.

Nick (age 33)

Self-confidence is also important:

Every day brings a new challenge when you are in this type of relationship. I believe the greatest challenge is to maintain the relationship once you have it. Insofar as opportunity is concerned, once you enter into your partner's world, especially if he has a strong personality, that really becomes your world outside of your own family. This doesn't always bring new opportunities, but in my own case it did. Ironically enough, it brought a career change which I had never anticipated. But most importantly, the woman has to have a very positive demeanor. Self-confidence is a major contribution to any healthy relationship, of any age, since it makes your partner respond to you in a positive manner.

Bobbi (age 51)

If a woman can just relax and let herself be, she can experience a whole different type of relationship. But she has to feel pretty secure and really like herself. That's the only way it can work.

Joel (age 34)

I had been told by a friend that something must be wrong with me...that obviously I didn't think very well of myself to be involved with a man so much younger. But really, the opposite was true. And I find the other women

I know who have done this are very confident and secure as well. You have to be, because the challenges are greater in this type of relationship.

Sharon (age 48)

We completely agree with Sharon. What seems to many to be a simple matter involving two people who choose to love one another is, in reality, a far more complex issue. Whereas many individuals are led to believe that their choice of romantic partner implies weakness and dysfunction, the truth is quite the opposite. Both the older woman and the younger man must possess a great degree of self-esteem and courage for, more than any of their other qualities and characteristics, these will be tested.

Chapter 24

Men Speak

I'd do it again...definitely, no question. Oh yeah, and once you've done it, you definitely look at older women in another way.
Nick (age 33)

We've made our position known and shared the thoughts and experiences of the women to whom we talked. Now it's time to let the men speak for themselves. One important question we asked was what they felt an older woman has to offer. Here are some answers which are clear, articulate and to the point. Their sentiments represent a very large proportion of the opinions we heard expressed.

I met Karolina at a party given by some friends. When I saw her, I thought she was just the perfect woman for me and I was sure about that. I wasn't looking for an older woman and Karolina wasn't looking for a younger man, but it just happened. (I was thirty-nine and she was fifty-five then). Our relationship is unique, because it's not just built on sex, but on trust, respect and love. We are both morning people and nearly always in a good mood. We are both hard-working with many hobbies in common. In my opinion, age has nothing to do with our relationship. In our twenty-five years together, we have never had a serious problem and we are still very happy.
Paolo (age 64)

Pat is very special. Not only is she beautiful, but she has a wonderful sense of humor and is very giving. The ability to talk about anything with her was refreshing and engaging. In fact, when I first met her, I didn't know I was attracted to an "older" woman. I knew she was older than I, but I didn't real-ize the disparity in age until she told me (which didn't happen until a couple of dates into our relationship). Pat offered me space, devotion and herself, which I couldn't find in anyone else. I take better care of myself now. She is a best friend who reflects back to me what a good person I am, which builds my confidence and self-esteem. I now have a better job and feel better about myself than ever before.

Neil (age 35)

Nigel, at thirty-seven, finds himself attracted to older women, in part for their clarity and substance and also their relaxed attitude about life:

I find that I'm attracted to a woman who has some degree of self-pos-session. I like the stimulation of a sharp intellect. I enjoy sitting down to din-ner with someone who has a level of conversation I can appreciate and enjoy.

I think younger women are sometimes focused too much on starting families and that is rarely an issue with older women. I've always had rela-tionships with older women. They know themselves. They have so much more to offer and they are looking for different things. They are not just looking for guys who will be good fathers and providers.

Older women can be more playful. They are more relaxed. It's really a personality thing for me regarding what is attractive. I enjoy a confident atti-tude and older women definitely have the upper hand in that area.

Dan, age twenty-four, also expressed a similar theme:

When I meet a woman over thirty, she's usually very clear and focused. She knows what she wants in life and it makes being with her so much easier. I look at a lot of my friends who have girlfriends their age and younger and the problems they have strike me as ridiculous. They frequently act foolish and immature. I don't have time for that behavior—that's why I like mature women.

That life experience is sexy was also a repeated theme:

Just the fact that there's so much to learn from an older woman, that they have so many more life experiences to draw upon, is an adventure to me. It's like a rush.

Vincent (age 31)

Some young men saw themselves reflected back in an older woman and realized the woman's own specialness:

She was very beautiful and caring and we had similar interests. She offered me the opportunity to see another perspective on a lot of different issues. I mean, older women think differently on certain issues and they've got more experience.

I grew up a lot with her. Yeah, definitely, she helped me to grow up. She made me realize how important I could be in making someone else happy. Not that I was doing it for her, but just by being with her.

Art (age 27)

Fred, age twenty-eight, told us what qualities attracted him to older women:

The experiences in life that they've had make them more grounded and realistic.

When asked what a mature woman offered him that he couldn't find in a younger woman, Fred answered:

Emotional stability. Need I say more? There have been nothing but positives in my relationships with two older women. They were able to see things in me that I could not see in myself. Also, there were levels of honesty unlike anything I've experienced even with best friends.

Fred gave us a wealth of information over several interviews. Open, upbeat and extremely handsome, he revealed the enormous love and respect he shared with his former partner and now shares with his current partner.

Fred's first older-woman experience occurred when he was twenty-one years old and Gretchen was thirty-seven. They lived together for two years. They are both still very close and see each other regularly. Not only did they have a tremendous friendship as the basis of their relationship, but an extraordinary sex life as well.

Recently, this woman underwent major surgery and it was her exboyfriend Fred, not the woman's current older boyfriend, who was by her side. Gretchen, now forty-four, was involved with a man of fifty-one and he was simply too busy with work and personal commitments to be available when she really needed him. It was Fred who visited her on a regular basis and saw to it that she had what she needed during her recuperation.

After his relationship with Gretchen ended, Fred tried dating girls in their early twenties. He explained, often quite humorously, how ridiculous he felt trying to have a meaningful conversation over blaring music at a dance club. His brief experimentation with younger females only reaped endless head games, confusion and immature behavior. Resolutely, Fred abandoned the "young woman trial period." He knew he liked older women and that was his standard. He decided this time to accept it.

His next relationship was with Marla, a co-worker. They were great friends and then she began to pursue him. *Why not?* he thought. *She was older. Maybe it would work.* But Marla's flaw seemed to be that she was only five years older—and for Fred, that still wasn't enough to produce the kind of emotional maturity and depth for which he searched.

After a year or so of taking a "time-out," Fred met Lynne. She is ten years older. Fred's respect and appreciation of older women was clear when he spoke:

> *The way mature women carry themselves shows they know who they are. It equates to stability. They've already figured out who they are. Maybe not all the time, but a lot more often than younger women. They are all-around much more attractive to me.*
>
> *Also, they are much more experienced with life. You know this is the kind of person who's going to tell you exactly what they want and they are more sure of themselves than the people my age or younger. Older women are much more well rounded—they know what they feel and why they feel it.*
>
> *It's easier to have a relationship with an older woman, because she knows how to communicate what she wants. It has a snowball effect all the way around.*
>
> *I have a preference for women starting at about ten years older than myself and up. It's adventurous for both of us, because it's a whole new exciting journey. Younger women just don't allow me to grow in the ways older women do.*

Not all older women/younger men relationships last forever, but Fred's answer to how he handled the ending of his relationship with an older woman was especially insightful:

> *I went on with my life and took with me many memories and experiences that made me mentally and emotionally rich. I considered it a hell of a jump-start on life.*

Certainly, there are challenges for the men as well as the women in these relationships. For example, the issue of having or not having children came up repeatedly.

> *My first relationship with an older woman—I was twenty and she was thirty-six—lasted two and a half years. My second—I was twenty-eight and she was forty-one—lasted three years and we lived together for one year.*
>
> *The main thing that attracted me was the overall calm of an older woman. There is a frenetic energy with a younger woman that can be very exciting and very cute, but not for my personality.*

Neither of my relationships was about being mothered. Both women were professionals, very focused on their work lives and extremely confident and sure of themselves. That was very attractive to me.

Lenny (age 38)

Ultimately, Lenny's last relationship ended when he wanted children and his partner of forty-three did not.

Of course, the issue of "Will I want children later on?" has become a less significant challenge to relationships between older women and younger men than it has been in the past. In vitro fertilization by donor eggs and other reproductive methods have greatly changed the fertility prognosis for older women. Pregnancy at ages once reserved for "miracles" is now a medical possibility.

Other challenges for the younger men occurred in the form of disapproval and criticism from friends and colleagues similar, although not as severe, to what the older women experienced.

I got more of a reaction from men than women. The men my age and older were jealous that I was with her. They would look at me as if I had something they wanted and didn't have and, because I was younger, they reacted more strongly. And women my age disapproved of the relationship.

Every morning, I would wake up happy and feel like I had the world on a string. I guess some of these people thought I was trying to prove something—I wasn't. Our relationship just made me feel great. She was great! I was proud of who she was and what we had together.

Barry (age 26)

Overall, however, it seems that such criticism is not as big an obstacle for men in these relationships as for women. In fact, some men received support and admiration from peers and co-workers:

Friends and colleagues all admired my decision to have a relationship with a mature woman. They respected what I had with her, which was an emotional connection with an experienced, centered person. Most people's reactions have been good. There have been no negative attitudes or comments given to me that stick out in my head. Actually, many people have asked my partner and me for advice.

Patrick (age 34)

The men to whom we talked spoke about the advantages of being in relationships with older women in terms of the serenity and comfort, the growth opportunity and the honesty they were afforded. But more than any other advantage, they talked about the positive sexual relationships they experienced. They *all* commented that sex with older women was better.

Negatives? What negatives? I cried, I laughed, I went back for more. The advantages can be summed up in two words: intense marathon.

Zach (age 32)

Advantages of having sex with an older woman? Are you kidding? An older woman is more sure of herself and brings that to the relationship. She knows what she wants and how to communicate that to her partner. I like not having to worry about pregnancy and an unwanted child. I do not feel the desire to have one and the lack of anxiety over that issue is relieving. Lisa is also in her prime and we have the most intense sexual relations I have ever had.

Gary (age 39)

The biggest advantage is that they know what they want so there's no guesswork. You may try to please them and they'll tell you if it isn't working. I loved it. That's a turn on. Absolutely no negatives about sex...it was the best. The best!

Scott (age 25)

Phenomenal! The sex was important—but I was really concerned about what she needed and desired. She would take over and go from there. It made things a hell of a lot easier, because we were just there to have fun. It was like breaking through a major barrier that takes other people forever to figure out. There was a "click" sexually. It was easy and it was great!

Russ (age 29)

If I look at a girl in her twenties, I might find her attractive, but my thoughts are only on sex. I can't really do anything with her. She's not formed yet. She's like a lump of cold clay—very pretty clay—but still unshaped.

When I look at older women, I see real women. They feel like women. They are solid. Their bodies are solid. Their thoughts have solidified. A relationship with an older woman can be very rewarding.

Mel (age 32)

I learned how to make love to a woman. She took me by the hand and said, "Slow down." I mean, I was twenty—and at twenty you're just so happy to actually be doing it...you never think about how.

Rick (age 27)

The only reason I'm interested in young women is strictly physical—I haven't met one in the last year or two who has the maturity that I'm looking for these days. Older women have definitely changed my taste as to what I'm attracted to. With most young women, I'm bored to death. Bored to death.

Lenny (age 38)

In a relationship, there is an intellectual component, a grounding component and a physical component. The physical is very important for a man...the sexual side is a big thing. It makes sense when you think about it...the greatest sex in my life has been with older partners. Even when it's early on in the relationship, it's still much deeper.

Michael (age 35)

Fred, who was mentioned earlier, expressed his own fulfillment:

Although my initial fear was that I wouldn't be good enough sexually, my larger fear was that I'd overwhelm her—like call too many times a day or say one too many "I miss yous." Instead, our mutual pleasure went from one high to another.

Chapter 25

Looking for Love

I had joined a dating a service, but as I looked through the books of photos all I could think was that these were older men. Then I was shocked to realize that they were all around my age. They just looked so defeated, so beaten down...
Elaine (age 51)

In all our lives, there will most likely be a time when we find ourselves alone. Partners die, relationships end and people change. As women, no matter how much success, prestige, creative expression and stellar friendships we've achieved, most of us prefer companionship. But being older, we are different now. Many of us have learned to say no to what doesn't work and refuse to make choices out of fear. We have grown more selective and more discriminating.

When I hit my late thirties and early forties, there was a smaller percentage of available men in my age group. So I met a lot of men on their third or forth divorce who carried a lot of emotional baggage. Then the young guys in their twenties began coming on to me. So I had only these two extremes. Guess which one I picked?

Marilyn (age 45)

For those of us who grew up with an image of the "correct relationship" and found it lacking, the door in our mind that was firmly closed has now swung open. We are able to acknowledge that we are attracted to younger men. We have expanded our options for love and romance. What was once forbidden territory is now simply an addition to our breadth of selection.

What was once uncomfortable now feels natural, especially if we've already had a relationship with someone younger. Other people's opinions may not even matter to us any more. What we once perceived as censure now looks like harmless mouths flapping in the breeze. We pay them no mind.

Now what? How do we meet these younger men? What's the process? The answer is the same as for meeting anyone else. We live our lives, do what we love, remain open and maybe he'll be there.

For most of us there comes a point, somewhere after the age of about thirty-five, that the singles scene is one huge effort. For many women, the idea of getting dressed up and going out for a night of manhunting sounds exhausting and rather depressing. A good video accompanied by popcorn or a frozen yogurt sounds much more inviting. Let's face it. The singles dating scene is a lot of work. Smiling at men you find suffocating, pretending you're listening as someone drones on about himself, dancing, or trying to dance, on an overcrowded floor—it can be a nightmare. And for what? To meet a man? Even a young man? This doesn't sound like an enjoyable evening. Or how about the single adult version of your seventh grade dance scenario: awkward girls on one side of the room, awkward boys on the other. Both groups want to meet someone, but everyone is too uncomfortable and uptight to venture out and be vulnerable. Is this any way for an adult to spend an evening?

Ah, partnership. It's great when it's great. And it can feel terribly lonely to be without someone. But one thing we've learned—if it isn't right, it's better to go solo.

It's too bad, we think, that solo has taken such a bad rap, because it really isn't as miserable as being with the wrong man. Our society just doesn't seem to know what to do with single people so it feels sorry for them. Solo brings up sad images: the odd chair at the table; the woman who "should" be invited (because she's alone, poor thing) but everyone's too uncomfortable with her single state to add her to the mix. How many women do you know who've rushed into a relationship with Mr. Wrong just because the pressure of being alone was unbearable?

Being alone, even for a brief time, can be great. Being alone can give us the energy and the time we need to develop ourselves, to do the things we really want to do. Still, we'd all like to meet someone special. So what's a mature, modern woman to do?

Get out of the house. You're not going to meet anyone by sitting around at home. It takes getting out and getting involved, but only with those activities you love, the activities that enhance and support you. Do the things that add real quality to your life, that make you feel expansive and free. Go where you feel charged by the activity or the experience. Maybe he'll be there.

A lot of clever ideas about how to meet a man have been expressed. We're told to sign up for financial planning seminars (lots of men there!). We're urged to join organizations in which we have no real interest and to involve ourselves in worthy charities for which we have no genuine passion. We don't believe that these methods work for evolved and authentic women.

You cannot be real if you cannot be yourself. You cannot generate passion in an environment in which you have no real interest. If financial seminars are your thing, then go. You'll be there for the right reasons and you'll have a better chance of attracting the young man who is also there because of genuine interest. If you love to go to the gym, go there. You'll meet others like yourself who also want to invest in their health and well-being. If you love to dance or enjoy music, go where you can dance or listen. You'll attract someone who shares your rhythm. But when you go anywhere with a false agenda, you are likely to meet others who have false agendas, too.

If you like the arts: Go to the theater or to the opera or movies you really want to see. Join organizations that attract other like-minded souls. Above all, don't compromise yourself. Follow your heart and your passion. At least you'll enjoy what you're doing, whether you meet someone or not. Finding a guy by the end of the evening won't be the measure of success. A night of compromising your true interests while searching for the right man that ends with nothing is a double loss. Invest your time and energy in fully developing yourself. You can't lose that way. You can only come out a winner.

If you don't participate in the unique forms of entertainment that you enjoy and enrich your life, you may not find a relationship that will either.

May, age forty-three, admitted that she wasn't specifically looking for a younger man, but she faced a common dilemma. Having chosen a fundamental conservative Christian lifestyle, she seemed to be limited to meeting only unavailable men. With the church at the center of her social life, the men in her age group were almost all married. Divorced or otherwise single men were rare in that environment. Because of her strongly structured beliefs, the pool of prospective mates narrowed because going to clubs and bars was not an option. What was she to do?

May continued to do what she loved. She went to church-related classes and seminars. She went where she felt uplifted and happy. There she met twenty-six-year-old Darryl. The attraction was immediate on both sides. Because she and Darryl shared the same moral and religious values, they were able to internally acknowledge their sexual chemistry while choosing to focus on creating a friendship. Eight months later they married.

Then there was Andrea, age fifty, who had been single for two years and had tried every technique she knew to meet a man. She asked friends to set her up, tried going out to local watering holes and even joined a business networking organization. She employed these tactics specifically to meet men. That was her intention. After a year and a half, she was exhausted and demoralized. She had worked very hard at her project only to come up empty-handed.

She described to us the incredible resistance she felt, while still trying to "work through it." But the energy just wasn't there. The harder she tried the less it worked. She confessed that she finally gave up, regrouped and decided to forget the whole thing:

> I couldn't take another night out. I just couldn't take one more step. I got more and more depressed about the whole thing so I quit. I didn't take numbers I didn't want. I didn't "look" for guys. I met younger guys, but I think I must have turned them off. Nothing came of it.
>
> I stayed home for about two months. I cleaned my closets, did some painting in my apartment and read some books I'd been meaning to get to. I discovered it wasn't so bad. I don't know why I was so afraid of it.
>
> Then one day when I was walking my dog, I ran into John. He had just moved into my neighborhood. We chatted and it was no big deal. Our dogs played. That was it or so I thought at the time. He was cute and young. But I just didn't go there in my head.

Andrea went on to explain that this "running into John" became more frequent. They continued their conversations and learned more about each other. She still didn't have any designs on him. She just liked him and was comfortable being herself. One day, he asked if they could meet at the park so their dogs could play. She agreed. They have been seeing each other for several months now.

We can't manufacture meetings with available men and thinking that we can is an illusion. To create a real partnership with a man, try creating a real partnership with yourself first. Do what you love, be who you are and maybe he'll find you. In the meantime, you'll be having a great time.

We know that a lot of people do meet each other through specific resources such as personal ads, dating services and the Internet. If you are an older woman and you'd like to meet a younger man, we'd like to share some tips as well as cautionary notes about these processes.

Dating Services

> They told me he was tall, dark and handsome. When I met him, he was short, gray and old.
>
> **Connie (age 46)**

Typically, if you're in your twenties and thirties, dating services are willing to match you with a same age candidate. After forty, however, a shift occurs. Women over forty report to us that being matched with a man close to their age is nearly impossible. The presumption of the dating service seems to be that a woman of forty-five *should* be paired with a man fifty-five or older. This is due to both the preference expressed by men and the prevailing social code which supports it. Generally, men over forty are looking for a woman who is ten to fifteen years younger than themselves. One famous fashion model, popular in the seventies, told us:

> *In my twenties I was making crazy money. I was flying high and there were always men around. No one was serious, we were just having fun.*
>
> *In my thirties, work fell off. I still had some good accounts, but no more magazine covers. I married a much older man (thirty-two years older). I wanted some stability in my life. I loved him, but I wasn't in love with him. I thought it would develop. It didn't. We divorced four years later. I have no regrets—he was very good to me.*
>
> *Then in my forties, I was alone. I wanted to settle down and live a more normal life. I'd meet men, but nothing clicked. I decided to try a particular dating service. They were very expensive and very good (so I heard). They even examined my financial records over the previous three years.*
>
> *They were known to have top-drawer people, so I gave it a go. They sent me out with great guys—but they were all in their late fifties to mid sixties. I felt like I was back in my marriage. I told the service that I wanted to meet men my own age and was told, "That just isn't done—these men only want women in their twenties."*
>
> *I happen to be young inside and I like men my own age or younger. But "on paper" the guys wouldn't go for it—no matter who or what I was. I was furious. Why can they get away with it, but if I want the same thing I can't have it because I'm a woman?*
>
> **Amanda (age 45)**

One trend in singles matchings is the gatherings where men and women, wearing name tags, go to meet and mingle. They are then separated to determine who was interested in whom. While this is obviously a better way of allowing natural chemistry to prevail, these functions are still organized according to age. Groups are arranged according to age categories, twenties-thirties or thirties-forties, etc. Still, the prevailing consciousness demands or expects that we be attracted only to those in the "appropriate" age group, typically with the men on the older end of the spectrum allowed to choose from among the women at the younger end. The culturally imposed limitation is reinforced once again.

One couple to whom we spoke—Elaine, age fifty-one, and David, age thirty-nine—met at a singles weekend, which evidently didn't impose age restrictions. We suggest you seek out those services and organizations willing to organize events based on criteria other than age. When in doubt, ask. Express your concerns and specify what you want before attending.

Whether you join a dating service or choose to go to a singles event, find out in advance how the age situation is handled. Is the dating service prepared to set you up with a younger man if your interests are similar? Are they even aware that there are women who wish to be open to such relationships? Are there dating services in your area that specialize in so-called "non traditional" relationships? Stating that you are open to this kind of pairing will help you as well as open the door for others wishing to do the same thing. Older women/younger men relationships are becoming increasingly common, but can't really become part of the mainstream until dating services and singles organizations know they exist and recognize there is a market for them. So speak your truth. It sets us all free.

Personal Ads

> **Seeking Soul Mate.** *SWM, 52, successful surgeon. Intelligent, iconclastic, well-read, world traveler. ISO sensuous, passionate beauty, model/actress/dancer type, 22-28, please be slim, curvaceous, well-endowed, 5'2" - 5'5" (105-115 lbs.), NS, D+D free.*

From whatever angle we approach them, personal ads present a peculiar set of problems. Notice the personal ads placed by men who are over forty. Many of them are quite specific in requiring that the woman be at least ten years younger, slender, shapely, sweet and lovely.

While we think that women should have as much right as men to request a much younger partner, it's a request that's all too often misconstrued. A forty-plus woman who advertises to meet a twenty-five-year-old guy will be viewed as a sex-obsessed older woman looking for a stud. Women need to be especially cautious when placing—or responding to—personal ads.

Personal ads are creatures all unto themselves. They force an instant intimacy that isn't an outgrowth of chemistry. Specific, detailed personal information is immediately disclosed. The process distorts the natural time frame of learning about a person. Much is revealed right away, but very little is really known. Time is condensed, disallowing the natural process to unfold. One just doesn't know who's on the other end of a personal ad or how they are interpreting our stated desire to meet someone younger. We know why we would like a younger man, but will he?

What about a man who advertises seeking a much older woman? Might there be an ulterior motive? Is he looking for a meal ticket or does he need an inordinate amount of nurturing? When people meet each other through personal contact, they are drawn to each other through a more natural process of mutual attraction and mutual interests. They see an individual as an entire package. They are attracted and then, at some point, they come to realize that they happen to be at different ends of the age spectrum. The age thing isn't the main event. When specified in an ad, it is.

If you decide to place a personal ad, you might describe yourself as a "mature woman seeking mate thirty to fifty." That broadens the age range and informs a respondent that you're not twenty-five, giving him the choice to answer based on whatever else you write.

Telling Him Your Age

Should you or shouldn't you? It has been our observation that when a man is really interested in a woman, he doesn't ask—because he doesn't care. He can see that she is older, but he is attracted to whom she is. Generally it is the woman who, at some point, feels the need to tell him her age, as if this will flush out an unwilling candidate.

Men who find you interesting and attractive, but are merely curious, will ask right away. They're just checking. In that case you might respond with a simple, "Why do you ask?" It is, after all, a rude question for a first time or otherwise casual encounter.

> I was sitting at the bar waiting for my friend when this guy starts talking to me. I don't think it was more than fifteen minutes before he looks at me and asks, "How old are you?" He was about ten or fifteen years younger, but I was floored because he had been really complimenting me, checking me out. So I just looked at him and said, "What's your net worth?"
>
> **Stacy (age 41)**

Though it's not conventional wisdom, often it is the men who will lie about their age. Ken, one fellow we know of, wanted to date a woman so badly that he added nine years to his age, figuring she wouldn't go near him if he told the truth and admitted he was only twenty. Ken was right. His lie allowed several dates to take place before he confessed. By that time she was already enjoying his company and, though shocked, decided to continue seeing him.

Despite Ken's success, don't lie about your age. If you entice a younger man by deducting years, he will find out the truth eventually. Should you want to get into a serious relationship he will assume that if you've lied to him about his you can and will lie about other things. The lie will only come back to haunt you. Honesty breeds an honest relationship. Games breed games, manipulation breeds manipulation and most of us are past the age of wanting to play games. It robs us of our energy, a resource we're trying to conserve. We'd prefer the freedom to really be ourselves and be appreciated for who we are. We want true intimacy, which can only be achieved through honesty. The man who is really interested in and attracted to you knows you are older and really doesn't care about the exact number. If your being older is a problem for him, you had best reconsider him as a potential mate.

The Internet

Perhaps it is the uniquely impersonal nature of the Internet that enables people to reveal their real identities. Strangers can express who they are without fear of the censure, scorn and ridicule that might otherwise be directed at them. So we find it particularly interesting that on the Internet the notion of older women/younger men relationships being viable and workable is spreading. Increasing numbers of people are logging on to the ever-growing Websites dealing with this topic, giving their opinions and, in some cases, giving free advice and counseling to older women/younger men couples.

If you are interested in finding out more about this easily accessible resource, we suggest you log on to the websites Lovestories.com and Agelesslove.com. Chat with others who share your issues, express your own thoughts and feelings or get free advice from a column called "Age Gap Relationships." As always, be careful and use good judgment.

Chapter 26

The Truth
About Being Older

*Along with sagging skin comes a resource of twenty years
of knowledge. I just kept remembering who I was, what I
was—inside, not just outside. I told myself every day,
"You're fifty and fabulous." Over a period of time it sunk in.*
Doreen (age 53)

We know a person who firmly believes that a woman is all washed up and utterly incapable of attracting a great man once she's reached fifty. The thinking of a male chauvinist? No, a beautiful, radiant, sophisticated and charismatic forty-seven-year-old woman. Dawn has been persuaded (as have many women) that once you hit fifty, the game is over. (In fact, one study chillingly warned that a woman over the age of thirty-five had a better chance of being killed by a terrorist's bullet than of finding a husband.) Dawn cites numerous examples of other women, once young and beautiful, who now at age fifty or older must settle for someone they never would have chosen in their earlier years. The reasoning behind this willingness to settle is the fear of being alone and the belief that having any man is better than having no man at all.

This is what we call a horror story. It is based on a belief that has been perpetuated by our society and passed down through generations of women, growing more frightening with each person it touches. There are certainly times in our lives, especially when we're feeling down, that this particular horror story becomes easier to believe. How often have we been at a gathering and observed a group of mature women commiserating with each other about the lack of available men? How often is this notion reinforced on popular television shows, in magazines and films? Are we really just like our cars? The end value based on an odometer reading, regardless of the condition or how loaded the vehicle? The *truth* is: It's only true if we believe it to be true.

When we were young girls, many of us felt middle age was thirty-five. Older women didn't look or live the way they do today. There were no concepts like the fabulous forties, the fantastic fifties and the successful sixties. Today, however, women look and feel better than ever and have more resources with which to improve their lives. More and more women are blossoming in their fifties and sixties and there is no reason love can't happen at any age. It is not reserved for the young. Listen to and read stories about women who have found the love of their life well into their later years. It happens more often than we are led to believe. Society, however, won't evolve in its belief about mature women until we do.

We have an attractive friend who just got engaged to the love of her life. Her age? Thirty-five? No. Forty-five? No. She is fifty-three. After two marriages—one as a very young woman and one in her thirties—she's now at a point where she has more to offer than ever before. We met her fiancé and he adores her. He too has come to a point in life where he is totally ready for partnership in a deeper, more meaningful way. Another woman we know just recently married. Her husband is forty; she is fifty-five. This is his first marriage. He told us that while he had known many women, he had decided not to marry until he met his soul mate. He did that, not caring a bit that she was fifteen years his senior.

If we think age is a curse, it will be. But age refines us, brings us to our fullness as individuals and allows us to be more complete and whole—if we've worked on ourselves and allowed ourselves to change and grow from life's experiences.

Growing up can also mean evolving into our true, mature selves. The fear that if we develop ourselves too much the pool of suitable men will diminish is a fallacy. It just means we will find another type of mate, one who better complements our own development. The truth is, *we* become more selective. Why should we fear becoming our real selves? Are we afraid "they" (men) won't like or love us if we do? Maybe they'll love us more.

Older women have made plenty of mistakes, taken lots of risks and know that perfection is a burden, not a desired state. They no longer hold their tongues; rather, they begin to express themselves in a rich way. They realize that they no longer need to protect others from hearing the truth, from understanding the nature and breadth of their needs and desires. They are, quite simply, more clear in their communication, more comfortable in their

own skin and guess what? Everyone—well maybe not everyone, but at least those who count—likes them!
Dr. Kathleen Calabrese

Our real value—and attractiveness—goes beyond our physical appearance. As an older woman you may be drop-dead gorgeous or consider yourself average. Whether you have a shapely body from hours spent on the Stairmaster or are totally out of shape, your ability to attract people is beyond all that. In our youth-obsessed culture, we tend to discount our true power. We've been sucked into believing that our value lies in our physical appearance. We've been so caught up in this concept that we've missed seeing the real truth.

It takes time for a woman to realize her value. As women age, they become more courageous, more audacious, bolder, less concerned about looks and more committed to all forms of fullness enriching their lives.
Dr. Kathleen Calabrese

In the past, youth and beauty have, unfortunately, been the primary measuring sticks for a woman's attractiveness.

Along with sagging skin comes a resource of twenty years of knowledge. I just kept remembering who I was, what I was—inside, not just outside. I had to force myself to look at the whole picture—not the male dominated cultural standard of weights and measurements—but the real picture. I told myself every day, "You're fifty and fabulous." Over a period of time it sunk in.
Doreen (age 53)

There is a balance in all of this. I just had to find it and hold onto it. It's not an easy job, but if I can do it, other women can, too. Being real inside, being comfortable with myself, being whole and complete—I think that's worth a lot. I focused on my assets and accepted my liabilities, then Mark suddenly popped into my life.
Sylvia (age 57)

Is it really true that our value is only physical? Or do we just collectively believe it to be true, giving it power by our beliefs? Do you remember the crushes you had on your college professors? They were older and so very intelligent (you thought then). Think about older men in your business or social sphere who have achieved great things and been successful. There is something very sexy and very seductive about knowledge and power, in women no less than in men.

When a person has matured and acquired her own identity and fullness as an individual, the landscape broadens. There is a richness and substance usually not found in younger souls. We see this happening all around us. Younger men are continuing to discover the many benefits of involvement with older women. There is a wonderful mystical quality and powerful dynamism between a young man and an older woman. He loves all of her, taking in the whole picture. Dr. Calabrese agrees:

> *They like this wonderful creature who is so easy to talk to, so much fun, so smart, so caring, so wise. Are we then surprised that a younger man might find this kind of woman incredibly sexy and intriguing? Are we at all surprised that an older woman, in some ways younger than ever, would know, in her heart, that a relationship with a younger man would suit her well? Not if you really think about it. Actually, it makes all the sense in the world. Do you think that the great queens and ancient goddesses took older men as lovers or mates? Not usually, and there is a reason for that. Think about it.*

Navigating our way through the uncharted waters of older women/younger men relationships has previously been hit or miss. There were no guidebooks or emotional maps and our mothers certainly never prepared us for this type of romance. But we are older now and our faith in ourselves has grown. We are proving daily that these years can truly be the best years of our lives.

Bibliography

De Madariaga, Isabel. *Catherine the Great: A Short History*. New Haven: Yale University Press, 1993.

Fein, Ellen, and Sherrie Schneider. *The Rules: Time Tested Secrets for Capturing the Heart of Mr. Right*. New York: Warner Books, 1996.

Friedan, Betty. *Feminine Mystique*. New York: W.W. Norton & Company, 1997.

Laumann, E., Paik, A., and Rosen, R. "Sexual Dysfunction in the United States: Prevalence and Predictors." Journal of the American Medical Association 281, no. 6 (February 10, 1999): 537-544.

Pittman, Frank. "Beware Older Women Ahead." *Psychology Today* 32, no. 1 (January 1999): 60.

Walker, Alexander. *Audrey: Her Real Story*. New York: St. Martin's Press, 1994.

Wolf, Naomi. *Beauty Myth: How Changes of Beauty Are Used Against Women*. New York: Doubleday, 1992.

Wolfe, Thomas. *The Web and the Rock*. Baton Rouge: Louisiana State University Press, 1999.

_____. *You Can't Go Home Again*. New York: HarperCollins, 1998.